Scotland

Atlantic
Ocean

SHETLAND

ORKNEY

HEBRIDES

SCOTLAND

North
Sea

N.
IRELAND

REPUBLIC
OF
IRELAND

WALES

ENGLAND

London

English Channel

FRANCE

HarperCollins*Publishers*

YOUR COLLINS TRAVELLER

Your Collins Traveller Guide will help you find your way around your holiday destination quickly and easily. It is split into two sections which are colour-coded:

The blue-coded 'topic' section comprises a series of excursions, presented in a clear and informative way, which can be followed round Scotland in a clockwise direction from Gretna Green, though of course it is possible to follow individual excursions too. The map on the inside front cover of this guide shows the main towns through which the excursions go, while a more detailed map is provided at the beginning of each route. However, it is recommended that you use the guidebook maps in conjunction with an up-to-date road atlas. Details of **ATTRACTIONS** and **RESTAURANTS** are also given for both Edinburgh and Glasgow, telling you how to get to them, what they will cost, when they are open and what to expect, as well as a **WALK** in each city. Each topic has its own simplified map, showing the position of each item and the nearest landmark or transport access, for instant orientation.

The red-coded section is a lively and informative gazetteer. In one alphabetical list you can find essential facts about the main places and cultural items – 'What is a broch?', 'Who was Rob Roy?' – as well as practical and invaluable travel information. It covers everything you need to know to help you enjoy yourself and get the most out of your time away, from Accommodation through Car Hire, Food, Health, Money, Newspapers, Taxis and Telephones to Youth Hostels.

Cross-references: Type in small capitals – **EDINBURGH-RESTAURANTS** – tells you that more information on an item is available within the topic on Edinburgh restaurants. A-Z in bold – **A-Z** – tells you that more information is available on an item in the gazetteer. Simply look under the appropriate heading. A name in bold – **Fort William** – also tells you that more information on an item is available in the gazetteer under that particular heading.

Packed full of information and easy to use – you'll always know where you are with your Collins Traveller Guide!

CONTENTS

CONTENTS

RED SECTION

INTRODUCTION

A professor of Spanish was on holiday in Scotland's Western Isles. One evening, in a bar, he got into conversation with a local schoolteacher about their respective languages, and asked if there was an equivalent in Gaelic for the Spanish word, *mañana*. The teacher thought for a while, and then replied, 'No, no. I do not think there is a word in the Gaelic that communicates such a pressing sense of urgency.'

An apocryphal story perhaps, but one which neatly sums up the relaxed pace of life in the Scottish Highlands and Islands, and the gentle humour of the inhabitants, just two of the many aspects of this fascinating country that make Scotland a popular holiday destination for visitors from all over the world.

However, this small, rugged country on the northwestern fringe of Europe suffers from something of an identity crisis. Many first-time visitors arrive with images of bagpipes, tartan and tins of shortbread, heather, haggis and Highland cows. This is the Scotland that is sold in souvenir shops. It is a mythical Scotland that grew out of the 19th century's romanticizing of the past, and from the stereotyped images of Scotland and the Scots portrayed by music hall acts like Harry Lauder and films such as *Brigadoon*. Outside the films and the souvenir shops, however, it is a Scotland that just doesn't exist. Fortunately, the real Scotland is not hard to find – all you have to do is go there and look around you. You will find a country of great scenic beauty, with some of the last real wilderness regions left in all of Europe; a country of genuine historic interest, rich in prehistoric sites, kirks, castles and battlefields, all evocative of its turbulent

IN LOYAL REMEMBRANCE
OF
ROBERT THE BRUCE
KING OF SCOTS
WHOSE VICTORY IN THIS
GLEN OVER AN ENGLISH
FORCE IN MARCH 1307,
OPENED THE CAMPAIGN OF
INDEPENDENCE WHICH HE
BROUGHT TO A DECISIVE
CLOSE AT BANNOCKBURN
ON 24TH JUNE 1314.

and eventful past; a country of practical, hard-working, generous people, reserved but welcoming, with a strong sentimental streak and a fierce pride in their homeland. This strong sense of national identity has been forged through a thousand years of conflict, mainly with the 'Auld Enemy', England. Since the disparate tribes of northern Britain first united under King Kenneth mac Alpin in AD 843, there have been many occasions when Scotland has had to fight to avoid being swallowed up by her larger neighbour, a struggle which has produced romantic heroes like William Wallace, Robert the Bruce and Bonnie Prince Charlie. The fight was apparently lost in 1707, when the Treaty of Union incorporated the Scottish parliament into Westminster, thus creating the United Kingdom. Theoretically, Scotland ceased to exist as a separate nation, but it preserved its own distinctive legal and educational systems, and there has been a strong undercurrent of discontent ever since, manifested in the Jacobite uprisings of 1715 and 1745, the Disruption in the Church of Scotland in 1843, and more recently in the electoral successes of the Scottish National Party in the 1970s, the general elections of the 1980s where the majority of Scots have consistently voted against the ruling Conservative Party, and in present-day opinion polls showing overwhelming support for increased self-determination.

And, of course, there is continued (mostly good-natured) rivalry between the two nations on the sporting field. There are few things a Scot enjoys quite as much as the rare pleasure of seeing his national team give the English a good thrashing at football or rugby.

Another story – an American tourist ducks into a shop doorway in Glasgow to avoid a downpour and remarks to a local standing there, 'Gee, how can you put up with all this terrible weather?' The Glaswegian replies, 'It's weather like this that's made the Scottish people what they are today.' 'What – dour, determined pragmatists?' asks the American. 'Naw, naw,' says the local, '. . . emigrants!'

Indeed, it has been said that Scotland's biggest export is its people. There are an estimated 20 million Scots scattered around the world, mainly in England, Canada, the USA, Australia and New Zealand. But it has rarely been the weather that has driven them from their homes. In the 18th and 19thC, it was the decision of landowners to turn over their estates to sheep farming and deerstalking that led to the notorious eviction of thousands of crofters, known as The Clearances. Most of the displaced farmers took ship to the New World, leaving behind the deserted communities of ruined blackhouses that can still be seen in many parts of the Highlands. The Depression of the 1930s and the post-war slump in traditional industries saw more recent waves of emigration. Today, the situation is slowly improving and new industries like tourism and fish farming are slowing the depopulation of the Highlands and Islands, while low property prices and a high quality of life are attracting many southerners. You will hear plenty of English accents during your trip to Scotland.

Historically, its people have been Scotland's greatest asset. Although it accounts for less than 10% of the population of Great Britain, it has produced more than 20% of its best philosophers, scientists, engineers

and inventors. This diminutive country's legacy to the world is out of all proportion to its size: Scots have pioneered the modern disciplines of political economy (Adam Smith), sociology (Adam Ferguson), geology (James Hutton and Charles Lyell) and electromagnetic theory (James Clerk Maxwell); the invention of the steam engine (James Watt), the pneumatic tyre (James Dunlop), the tarred roadway (John Macadam), the telephone (Alexander Graham Bell) and the television (John Logie Baird); the early development of anaesthesia (James Young Simpson), the petroleum industry (James 'Paraffin' Young) and antibiotics (Alexander Fleming); of course, there is the much-loved literature of Robert Burns, Sir Walter Scott and Robert Louis Stevenson, read and enjoyed all over the world; and who can claim never to have sung *Auld Lang Syne*, penned by Burns in the 18thC?

Scotland's famous figures and eventful history are well documented in its many museums, castles and monuments, ranging from huge establishments like the Royal Scottish Museum in Edinburgh to tiny village museums occupying a single room in a cottage. Such places are welcome indoor attractions in a country that is notorious for its foul weather. Scotland's soggy reputation is, however, overstated. It results from

most tourists visiting the country in July and August, which are consistently the wettest months of the year, and spending most of their time in the west, which is the wettest area. May, June and September often enjoy mild, sunny weather, and springtime has the added bonus of bluebell woods and rhododendrons in full bloom. And simply driving for 60 miles or so from the west to the east coast will deposit you in a warmer and drier summer climate.

It is contrasts like this, squeezed into such a compact and accessible area, that account for much of Scotland's charm. Only a few hours' drive from Edinburgh you can roam amid the starkly beautiful scenery of the Cairngorm and Grampian mountains. Rare alpine plants grow on mountain tops less than 50 miles from a coast warmed by a branch of the Gulf Stream, where open-air gardens support species normally confined to the tropics. In the space of a few days, you could enjoy experimental drama in one of Glasgow's theatres, play golf on a world championship course, explore a 4500-year-old Neolithic village and watch a spectacular sunset from a deserted sweep of surf-pounded sand.

Scotland is an intriguing and addictive country – many visitors return year after year and never tire of its attractions. It is a country that delights not only visitors from abroad, but also its native inhabitants. Their pride is reflected in the Scots' toast to themselves: 'Here's tae us, wha's like us? Damn few, and they're a' deid!'

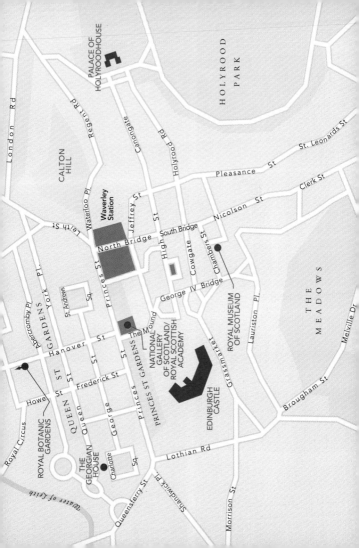

EDINBURGH CASTLE High St.
❑ 0930-1750 Mon.-Sat., 1030-1645 Sun. (April-Sep.); 0930-1620
Mon.-Sat., 1230-1535 Sun. (Oct.-Mar.). ❑ £2.80, child £1.40.
Dating back to the 12thC, the castle dominates the city: see St.
Margaret's Chapel, the Great Hall and Mon's Meg (15thC cannon).

PALACE OF HOLYROODHOUSE Canongate.
❑ 0930-1715 Mon.-Sat., 1030-1630 Sun. (April-Sep.); 0930-1545
Mon.-Sat. (Oct.-Mar.). ❑ £1.60, child 80p.
Royal family's official Scottish residence, dating back to the 15thC; has
links with Mary, Queen of Scots, Bonnie Prince Charlie and George IV.

NATIONAL GALLERY OF SCOTLAND The Mound.
❑ 1000-1700 Mon.-Sat., 1400-1700 Sun. ❑ Free.
One of the best small European galleries; fine Impressionists collection.

ROYAL SCOTTISH ACADEMY The Mound.
❑ 1000-1900 Mon.-Sat., 1400-1700 Sun. ❑ £1.20, child 50p.
Built to a Greek Temple design in 1826. Exhibits renowned artists.

ROYAL MUSEUM OF SCOTLAND Chambers St.
❑ 1000-1700 Mon.-Sat., 1400-1700 Sun. ❑ Free.
Decorative arts, archaeology, technology, etc. Lovely glass-roofed hall.

THE GEORGIAN HOUSE 7 Charlotte Sq.
❑ 1000-1700 Mon.-Sat., 1400-1700 Sun. (April-Nov.). ❑ £2.20.
Georgian town house (c.1800), lovingly restored in every detail.

ROYAL BOTANIC GARDENS Inverleith Row.
❑ 0900-1 hr before sunset Mon.-Sat., 1100-1 hr before sunset Sun.
(Mar.-Oct.); 0900-dusk Mon.-Sat., 1100-dusk Sun. (Nov.-Feb.). ❑ Free.
A variety of gardens and the UK's largest collection of rhododendrons.

CALTON HILL East end of Princes St.
328 ft hill topped by the unfinished, twelve-columned National
Monument, the 100 ft Nelson Monument and the City Observatory.

Restaurants

THE HOWTOWDIE 24a Stafford St.
❏ 1200-1400, 1900-2300 Mon.-Fri., 1900-2300 Sat. ❏ Expensive.
Traditional Scottish cooking served in one of the city's best restaurants.

L'AUBERGE 56-58 St. Mary's St.
❏ 1215-1400, 1845-2130. ❏ Expensive.
Genuine nouvelle cuisine is served in this stylish French restaurant.

CAFÉ ROYAL OYSTER BAR 17a West Register St.
❏ 1200-1400, 1900-2230. ❏ Expensive.
The oldest seafood restaurant in Scotland. Interesting Victorian interior.

JACKSON'S 2 Jackson's Close, 209 High St.
❏ 1200-1500, 1800-2230 Mon.-Sat. ❏ Moderate.
Elegant restaurant; the menu shows Scottish and French influences.

NEW EDINBURGH RENDEZVOUS 10a Queensferry St.
❏ 1200-1400, 1730-2330 Mon.-Sat., 1300-2330 Sun. ❏ Moderate.
Sample some of the best Pekinese cuisine in Scotland.

HENDERSON'S SALAD TABLE 94 Hanover St.
❏ 0800-2300 Mon.-Sat. ❏ Moderate.
Popular, self-service restaurant offering a huge selection of salads.

THE DORIC 5 Market St.
❏ 1200-0100 Mon.-Wed., 1200-0200 Thu.-Sat., 1830-2300 Sun.
❏ Inexpensive-Moderate.
Bar and bistro serving a wide range of appetizing dishes.

KALPNA 2-3 St. Patrick's Sq.
❏ 1200-1400, 1730-2330 Mon.-Sat. ❏ Inexpensive-Moderate.
A southern Indian, non-smoking, vegetarian restaurant.

BAR ITALIA 100 Lothian Rd.
❏ 1700-0230. ❏ Inexpensive.
Excellent pizzas and pasta dishes; ideal for hungry late-night revellers.

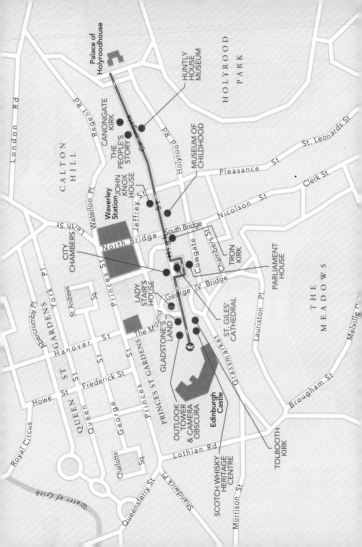

Palace of Holyroodhouse

HUNTLY HOUSE MUSEUM

HOLYROOD PARK

London Rd

Regent Rd

CANONGATE KIRK

Canongate

Holyrood Rd

MUSEUM OF CHILDHOOD

St. Leonards St

Pleasance

CALTON HILL

THE PEOPLE'S STORY

JOHN KNOX HOUSE

Clerk St

Waterloo Pl

Waverley Station

Leith St

Jeffrey St

St Mary's St

Nicolson St

North Bridge

South Bridge

CITY CHAMBERS

Princes St

Cowgate

Chambers St

TRON KIRK

PARLIAMENT HOUSE

LADY STAIR'S HOUSE

The Mound

George IV Bridge

ST. GILES' CATHEDRAL

THE MEADOWS

GLADSTONE'S LAND

Lauriston Pl

Abercromby Pl

York Pl

St Andrews Sq

Hanover St

Frederick St

Princes St Gardens

PRINCES ST GARDENS

Melville Dr

OUTLOOK TOWER & CAMERA OBSCURA

Edinburgh Castle

Grassmarket

Brougham St

Queen St

George St

Howe St

Charlotte Sq

Lothian Rd

TOLBOOTH KIRK

Royal Circus

SCOTCH WHISKY HERITAGE CENTRE

Morrison St

Queensferry St

Shandwick Pl

Water of Leith

Walk

The Royal Mile. Duration: 2-4 hr.

This historic thoroughfare links two of the city's main tourist attractions, the Castle (see **EDINBURGH-ATTRACTIONS**) and the Palace of Holyroodhouse (see **EDINBURGH-ATTRACTIONS**). There is much to see and the time required will depend on how many stops you make to visit the various museums and buildings.

Begin at the Castle Esplanade. On the right is Cannonball House (built 1630). The cannonball lodged in the wall was not fired in anger, but marked the gravitation height of the city's first piped water supply. Across the street is a fountain, dated 1722, which marks the spot where hundreds of women were burnt as witches. At the corner with Ramsay Lane is the Outlook Tower and Camera Obscura (1000-1800 April-Oct. 1000-1700 Nov.-Mar.; £2.50, child £1.25), while on the right is the Scotch Whisky Heritage Centre (1000-1900 April-Oct., 0900-1700 Nov.-Mar.; £2.85, child £1.50). As you descend Castlehill, the Tolbooth Kirk (1842-44) comes into view; its 240 ft tower is the tallest in Edinburgh. A few yards beyond the kirk on the left is Gladstone's Land (1000-1700 Mon.-Sat., 1400-1700 Sun., April-Oct.; £2, child £1), a six-storey tenement building dating from 1617, and through the neighbouring close you will find Lady Stair's House (1000-1800 Mon.-Sat., June-Sep., until 1700 Oct.-May; free), built in 1622, presented to the city in 1907 and now housing a literary museum. Cross George IV Bridge (a brass plaque in the roadway on the right-hand side marks the site of the city's last public execution in 1864) and turn right into Parliament Sq. Here you will find St. Giles' Cathedral (0900-1900 Mon.-Sat.; cathedral free, Thistle Chapel 30p, child 5p). A church has stood on the site since AD 854 but most of the present-day structure dates from 1829-33. The ornate Thistle Chapel was added in 1907-11. John Knox (see **A-Z**) was the minister here from 1559-72. Brass plaques in the cobblestones in front of the cathedral mark the outline of the Tolbooth (the old town gaol, demolished in 1817), while the Heart of Midlothian marks the site of the condemned cell. After visiting the Parliament House (0930-1630 Tue.-Fri.; free), leave the square at the Mercat Cross (which includes part of the original 15thC cross), opposite the splendid City Chambers, designed by John Adam in 1761. At the downhill end of the chambers

is Anchor Close, where in 1768 William Smellie printed the first edition of the *Encyclopaedia Britannica*. Further down the street, at the junction with South Bridge, stands the Tron Kirk, named after the tron or weighing machine that once stood on the spot, which dates from 1637. Beyond the bridges, on the left, is Paisley Close, with an inscription above the door which reads 'Heave awa' chaps, I'm no' deid yet', the words of a man who was rescued from a tenement collapse here in 1861. Downhill on the right is the Museum of Childhood (1000-1800 Mon.-Sat., June-Sep., until 1700 Oct.-May; free), and where the street narrows is the distinctive John Knox House

(1000-1700 Mon.-Sat., April-Oct., until 1600 Nov.-Mar.; £1, child 50p). At the junction with St. Mary's St and Jeffrey St more brass plaques mark the outline of the old Netherbow Port (built 1513, demolished 1764), one of the six gates in the old city wall. Its original appearance can be seen in a model on display in Huntly House Museum (see below). Continue down Canongate, passing on the right Chessel's Court, where Deacon Brodie was caught robbing the Excise Office and was subsequently hanged. Opposite Huntly House Museum (1000-1800 Mon.-Sat., June-Sep.; 1000-1700 Mon.-Sat., Oct.-May; free) is the Canongate Tolbooth and the museum illustrating the history of the local people: The People's Story (times as Huntly House Museum). Next to the tolbooth is Canongate Kirk (1688). The surrounding kirkyard contains the graves of Adam Smith (see **A-Z**) and the poet Robert Fergusson. Fergusson's headstone was erected by Robert Burns (see **A-Z**) and later renovated by R. L. Stevenson (see **A-Z**). Near the foot of the Canongate, on the left, is White Horse Close, a converted 17thC coaching inn which was once the departure point for the stagecoach to London. Cross the roundabout to Abbey Strand and finish your walk at the gates of the Palace of Holyroodhouse, which were erected in 1922 as part of a memorial to King Edward VII.

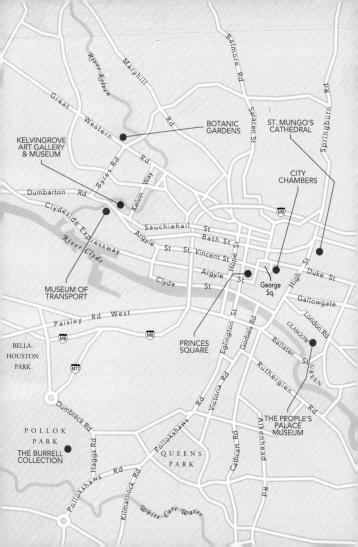

River Kelvin

Maryhill

Great Western Rd

Balmore Rd

Saracen St

Springburn Rd

BOTANIC GARDENS

ST. MUNGO'S CATHEDRAL

KELVINGROVE ART GALLERY & MUSEUM

Byres Rd

Rd

Kelvin Way

CITY CHAMBERS

Dumbarton Rd

Clydeside Expressway

River Clyde

Sauchiehall St

Bath St

Argyle St

St. Vincent St

Hope St

Argyle St

Duke St

M8

High St

MUSEUM OF TRANSPORT

Clyde St

George Sq.

Gallowgate

London Rd

Paisley Rd West

M8

Eglinton St

Gorbals Rd

Ballater St

GLASGOW GREEN

PRINCES SQUARE

BELLAHOUSTON PARK

M8

M77

Dumbreck Rd

Victoria Rd

Rutherglen Rd

Cathcart Rd

Aitkenhead Rd

THE PEOPLE'S PALACE MUSEUM

POLLOK PARK

THE BURRELL COLLECTION

Pollokshaws Haggs Rd

Pollokshaws Rd

Kilmarnock Rd

Pollokshaws Rd

QUEENS PARK

White Cart Water

KELVINGROVE ART GALLERY & MUSEUM Argyle St.
❑ 1000-1700 Mon.-Sat., 1400-1700 Sun. ❑ Free.
Built in 1902, it houses the finest civic art collection outside London.

THE BURRELL COLLECTION Pollokshaws Rd.
❑ 1000-1700 Mon.-Sat., 1400-1700 Sun. ❑ Free.
Sir William Burrell's collection of ancient Mediterranean art, Gothic tapestries, 19thC French paintings, etc., in an award-winning building.

THE PEOPLE'S PALACE MUSEUM Glasgow Green.
❑ 1000-1700 Mon.-Sat., 1400-1700 Sun. ❑ Free.
Glasgow's social and economic history; industry, religion, sport, etc.

MUSEUM OF TRANSPORT Kelvin Hall, Bunhouse Rd.
❑ 1000-1700 Mon.-Sat., 1400-1700 Sun. ❑ Free.
Collection of vintage cars, trains, model ships, etc., plus a 1930s 'street'.

ST. MUNGO'S CATHEDRAL Castle St.
❑ 0930-1300, 1400-1900 Mon.-Sat., 1400-1700 Sun. (April-Sep.); 0930-1230, 1330-1600 Mon.-Sat., 1400-1600 Sun. (Oct.-Mar.).
Present building dates from 13thC, built on the site of a 5thC Christian burial ground; has an impressive interior and notable West Window.

CITY CHAMBERS George Sq.
❑ Guided tours 1030 & 1430 Mon.-Wed. & Fri. ❑ Free.
Designed by William Young in Italian Renaissance style (1883-88). See the astonishing Council Hall, Banqueting Hall and various salons.

BOTANIC GARDENS Great Western Rd.
❑ Dawn-dusk; Kibble Palace 1000-1645 (winter till 1615); Glasshouse 1300-1645 (winter till 1615) Mon.-Sat., 1200-1645 Sun. ❑ Free.
The Kibble Palace is a Victorian glasshouse with ponds and sculptures.

PRINCES SQUARE Buchanan St.
❑ 1000-1900 Mon.-Sat., 1130-1630 Sun. Restaurants open till 2400.
Stylish shopping mall with a variety of unusual and expensive boutiques.

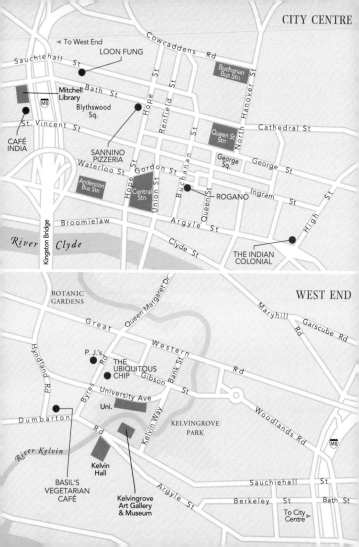

CITY CENTRE

To West End

Cowcaddens Rd

Sauchiehall St

LOON FUNG

Bath St

Mitchell Library

Blythswood Sq.

Hope St

Renfield St

Buchanan Bus Stn

North Hanover St

Cathedral St

CAFÉ INDIA

St. Vincent St

SANNINO PIZZERIA

Queen St Stn

George Sq.

George St

Waterloo St

Gordon St

Hope St

Anderston Bus Stn

Central Stn

Union St

Buchanan St

Queen St

ROGANO

Ingram St

High St

Broomielaw

Argyle St

River Clyde

Kingston Bridge

Clyde St

THE INDIAN COLONIAL

WEST END

BOTANIC GARDENS

Queen Margaret Dr.

Maryhill Rd

Garscube Rd

Great Western Rd

Hyndland Rd

P. J.'s

THE UBIQUITOUS CHIP

Bank St

Gibson St

Byres Rd

University Ave

Uni.

Kelvin Way

KELVINGROVE PARK

Woodlands Rd

Dumbarton Rd

River Kelvin

Kelvin Hall

BASIL'S VEGETARIAN CAFÉ

Kelvingrove Art Gallery & Museum

Argyle St

Sauchiehall St

Berkeley St

Bath St

To City Centre

Restaurants

ROGANO 11 Exchange Pl.
❏ 1200-1430, 1900-2230 Mon.-Sat. ❏ Expensive.
Exotic Art Deco interior and unique atmosphere. Specializes in succulent seafood dishes.

THE INDIAN COLONIAL 25 High St.
❏ 1200-1430 Mon.-Sat., 1800-2230 Tue.-Sat. ❏ Expensive.
Restaurant serving Indian cuisine, which aims to be the best of its kind in the country.

THE UBIQUITOUS CHIP 2 Ashton Lane.
❏ 1200-1430, 1730-2300 Mon.-Sat. ❏ Expensive.
Fashionable Scottish cuisine in a leafy courtyard setting; upstairs bar.

LOON FUNG 417 Sauchiehall St.
❏ 1200-2330. ❏ Moderate-Expensive.
The best Cantonese food in the city centre.

CAFÉ INDIA 171 North St.
❏ 1200-1430, 1700-2400 Mon.-Thu., 1200-2400 Fri. & Sat., 1700-2400 Sun. ❏ Moderate.
*Excellent curries; wide wine and beer selection (see **GLASGOW-WALK**).*

BASIL'S VEGETARIAN CAFÉ 184 Dumbarton Rd.
❏ 1200-2130 Sun., Mon. & Wed., 1830-2130 Tue., 1200-2300 Thu.-Sat. ❏ Inexpensive-Moderate.
Small licensed café specializing in vegetarian and vegan dishes.

SANNINO PIZZERIA 61 Bath St.
❏ 1200-2400 Mon.-Sat. ❏ Inexpensive-Moderate.
Superb pizzas and pasta at reasonable city centre prices.

P. J.'S Ruthven Lane.
❏ 1200-1430, 1700-2400 Mon.-Fri., 1200-2400 Sat. & Sun.
❏ Inexpensive.
Good quality, if rather unconventional, pasta dishes.

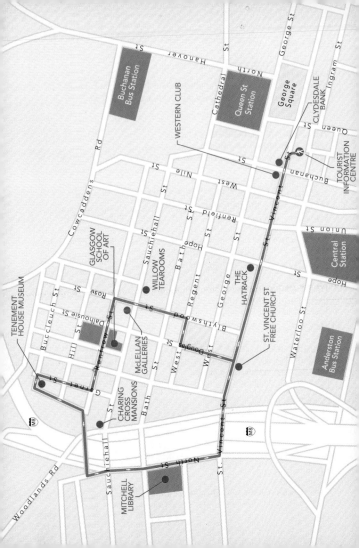

Walk

City Centre. Duration: 2 hr 30 min.

Start in St. Vincent Pl. beside the Tourist Information office. Opposite is the Clydesdale Bank (1870-73) by John Burnet, one of the finest examples of Palladian architecture in Europe. Walk along to the junction with Buchanan St. On the right-hand corner is the former Western Club (1840-41) by David Hamilton, perhaps his most notable building. Follow St. Vincent St up the hill. Just beyond the junction with Hope St on the right, at Nos 142-44, is the eight-storey building by James Salmon Jnr known as the 'Hatrack' (1899) because of its unusually tall and slim design. Beside it is the modern glass frontage of the Scottish Amicable building (1972-75). Continue up St. Vincent St, turn right into Douglas St and enter Blythswood Sq., designed in the 1820s by John Brash. Charles Rennie Mackintosh (see **A-Z**) designed the doorway of No. 5, which used to be the headquarters of the Glasgow Society of Lady Artists. Leave the square by Blythswood St, which leads onto Sauchiehall St pedestrian precinct, a favourite area for pavement artists. Turn right and a few yards further along are the Willow Tearooms (0930-1630 Mon.-Sat.), designed by Mackintosh for Miss Kate Cranston in 1903, and now restored to their original condition. From the tearooms, cross to the opposite side of Sauchiehall St and turn right into Rose St. On the left are the McLellan Galleries (1000-1700 Mon.-Wed., Fri. & Sat., 1000-2200 Thu., 1200-1800 Sun.), an international exhibition venue, and to the right the Glasgow Film Theatre. Turn left into Renfrew St. A short walk up the hill is the Glasgow School of Art (guided tours by appointment, tel: 041-3329797), Mackintosh's most celebrated building, built 1907-08. Continue along Renfrew St then turn right into Garnet St. Just over the hill turn left into Buccleuch St and ahead on the corner is the Tenement House Museum (1400-1700 Easter-Oct., 1400-1600 Sat. &

Sun., Jan.-Easter; £1, child 50p), a re-creation of a late 19thC family home. Turn the corner and take the right fork of the path ahead which slopes down the hill to rejoin Renfrew St. Cross the bridge over the M 8 motorway, turn left and walk down to Charing Cross past the drinking fountain. Cross at the traffic lights and stop to look back across the busy junction to Charing Cross Mansions (1889-91) by Burnet, Son and Campbell, an elaborately decorated tenement block with a baroque clock and carved figures. Follow North St, and on the right is the copper-domed Mitchell Library (0930-2100 Mon., Tue., Thu., Fri., 0930-1700 Sat.; free), built 1906-11, the largest civic-owned reference library in Europe. Carry on beside the M 8 motorway past Café India (see **GLASGOW-RESTAURANTS**) until you reach the junction with St. Vincent St. Turn left and walk up the hill. On the right is the BP Exploration building, which boasts a roof-terrace, and beside it is St. Vincent St Free Church (1858-59) by Alexander 'Greek' Thomson, the city's most original architect after Mackintosh. Note the tower which combines classical and Italianate design. Follow St. Vincent St back over the hill to St. Vincent Pl.

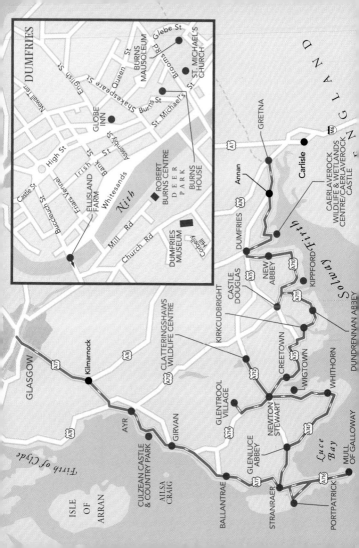

DUMFRIES

Glebe St

BURNS
MAUSOLEUM

Queen St

Rd

Brooms

ST. MICHAEL'S
CHURCH

English St

Shakespeare St

Newall Terr

Burns St

St. Michael's

High St

GLOBE
INN

Assembly St

Bank St

Irish St

ELLISLAND
FARM

Whitesands

Friars Vennel

Castle St

Buccleuch St

Nith

Mill Rd

Church Rd

ROBERT
BURNS CENTRE

DEER
PARK

BURNS
HOUSE

DUMFRIES
MUSEUM

Corbelly
Hill

ENGLAND

GRETNA

M6

A7

Annan

Carlisle

Dumfries

A74

CAERLAVEROCK
WILDLIFE & WETLANDS
CENTRE/CAERLAVEROCK
CASTLE

Solway Firth

NEW
ABBEY

A75

KIPPFORD

A710

CASTLE
DOUGLAS

A711

DUNDRENNAN ABBEY

KIRKCUDBRIGHT

CLATTERINGSHAWS
WILDLIFE CENTRE

A713

CREETOWN

A75

GLASGOW

A77

Kilmarnock

A76

GLENTROOL
VILLAGE

A714

LWIGTOWN

NEWTON
STEWART

WHITHORN

A746

AYR

A78

GIRVAN

CULZEAN CASTLE
& COUNTRY PARK

AILSA
CRAIG

A716

GLENLUCE
ABBEY

A75

Luce
Bay

Firth of Clyde

ISLE
OF
ARRAN

BALLANTRAE

STRANRAER

PORTPATRICK

A716

MULL
OF
GALLOWAY

Gretna Green–Glasgow. Duration: 3 days.

Gretna Green. The village is well signposted and easily reached from
the main north–south A 74 road. In times past young English lovers
would elope across the border to be married by the village blacksmith,
since up to 1940 Scots Law allowed couples over 16 to marry without
their parents' consent. The Smithy celebrates those times. Turn down
the road running south out of the village until you come to a T-junction, where you turn right onto the B 721.

1 mile – Gretna. Tourist Information (Easter-Oct.), Headless Cross,
tel: 0461-37834. Carry on along the main road to Annan. Pass through
the town and take the B 724 off to the left. After 13 miles turn left to
Ruthwell Church which contains the Ruthwell Cross, an 18 ft-high
cross dating from the 8thC and covered in elaborate runic carvings.
Rejoin the main road, turning left towards Bankend where you turn left
again, following the road to Dumfries.

21 miles – Caerlaverock Wildfowl & Wetlands Centre (0930-1700
Sep.-April; £2, child £1.10). A reserve famous for its population of bar-
nacle geese together with swans, ducks, oystercatchers and other
waders.

22 miles – Caerlaverock Castle (0930-1900 Mon.-Sat., 1400-1900
Sun.; 60p, child 30p). Built in the late 13thC this fascinating triangular-
shaped castle is amazingly well preserved. A complete water-filled
moat surrounds it while inside you can see the contrasting Renaissance
architecture which was added in the 17thC. Rejoin the B 725, running
parallel to the River Nith, through Glencaple.

30 miles – Dumfries (see **A-Z**). Leave the town and head southwest on
the A 710.

37 miles – New Abbey. Devorguilla Balliol, wife of John Balliol, established Sweetheart Abbey (0930-1900 Mon.-Sat., 1400-1900 Sun.; 60p,
child 30p) in 1273 in memory of her husband and was buried in front
of the altar together with his heart. John Balliol had himself earlier been
forced to become a benefactor of Oxford University, building the college that still bears his name, after being publicly flogged for 'damnify-
ing' the churches of Durham and Tynemouth. The red sandstone
church is surprisingly well preserved with beautifully sculpted arches,

columns and windows, though little of the monastery remains. The 30
acre site is encircled by a wall of vast boulders. Two hundred yards
along the Main St from the abbey is The Cornmill (0930-1900 Mon. &
Thu.-Sat., 0930-1200 Tue., 1400-1900 Sun.), a working water mill with
millpond and water wheel. Continue on the A 710.

48 miles – Sandyhills has an extensive, overly popular beach.
Continue along the A 710 then turn left for 1.2 miles.

54 miles – Rockcliffe. Rough Island, a bird sanctuary where tern and
oystercatchers nest on the shingle beaches, stands 200 yd offshore and
can be reached by boat, or walked at low tide if you like mud. You can
also walk through woods above the shore to Kippford (see below), past
the Mark of Motte, a 5th-7thC Celtic hill-top stronghold. Alternatively,
to reach the village by road, you can rejoin the A 710 and bear left,
continue for 2 miles, then turn left again.

57 miles – Kippford. A tiny village perched on the shore of the Rough
Firth. Brilliant food can be enjoyed at the Anchor Inn. Rejoin the
A 710, turning right. After 3 miles, turn left onto the A 711.

DETOUR: Turn right on the A 745 for 6 miles to Castle Douglas (Tourist
Information, Easter-Oct., Markethill, tel: 0556-2611) to visit Threave
Gardens (0900-sunset), set in 60 acres of beautiful grounds and, stand-

ing dourly on an island in the middle of the Dee, Threave Castle (1000-1300, 1400-1800 Mon.-Sat., 1400-1800 Sun., April-Sep.; 60p, child 30p), appropriately built in 1360-70 by Archibald the Grim, who hung his many victims from the prominent corbel in the battlements. Return to the A 711.

After half a mile turn left.

63 miles – Orchardton Tower (0930-1900 Mon.-Sat., 1400-1900 Sun.). A rare example of a circular 15thC tower house. Continue on the A 711.

71 miles – Dundrennan Abbey (0930-1900 Mon.-Sat., 1400-1900 Sun.). Built in 1142, this was the last place Mary, Queen of Scots (see **A-Z**) stayed in Scotland before fleeing to England in 1568, never to return. This Cistercian abbey has fine transepts and an interesting 13thC arched doorway to the chapterhouse. Follow the A 711 north past the MOD firing range.

77 miles – Kirkcudbright. Pop: 3500. Full services. Tourist Information (Easter-Oct.), Harbour Sq., tel: 0557-30494. The town looks as if it has been transported north from Cornwall, set as it is on an estuary dotted with fishing boats. Pronounced 'Kirk-coo-brie', the name derives from that of a 7thC Northumbrian monk, St. Cuthbert, who made numerous missionary expeditions to Galloway. McLellan's Castle (0930-1600 Mon.-Sat., 1400-1900 Sun., Mar.-Sep.; 80p, child 40p) on the waterfront was built in 1582 with stones from the old priory. Nearby on St. Mary's St is the Stewartry Museum (1100-1600 Mon.-Sat., Easter-Oct.; £1, child free), detailing local history and the life of John Paul Jones, founder of the American navy. On the High St lies Broughton House (1100-1300, 1400-1700 Mon. & Wed.-Sat., 1400-1700 Sun., Easter-Oct.; £1.50, child 50p), home of the painter E. A. Hornel (1864-1933), which now displays a collection of his work. Take the A 755 northwest out of town and, after 5.5 miles, turn left onto the A 75.

Salmon fishing, Creetown

85 miles – Cardoness Castle (0930-1900 Mon.-Sat., 1400-1900 Sun.; 60p, child 30p). On a crag at the turn-off to Gatehouse of Fleet, this 15thC tower house is noted for its original stairway and vaulted basement ceiling. Continue for 5.5 miles and turn right.

91 miles – Cairn Holy. There are two chambered cairns here dating back to 2000 BC. Rejoin the A 75 running alongside Wigtown Bay.

92 miles – Carsluith Castle (0930-1900 Mon.-Sat., 1400-1700 Sun.). A ruined four-storey L-plan tower house built in the 16thC.

96 miles – Creetown. The town itself is off the main road to the right, 1.3 miles away, and here can be found the Creetown Gem and Rock Museum (0930-1800; 80p, child 40p), an exhibition displaying a range of mineral forms from around the world. Rejoin the A 75.

101 miles – Newton Stewart. Pop: 3200. Full services. Tourist Information (Easter-Oct.), Dashwood Sq., tel: 0672-2431. The town gets its name from William Stewart, a son of the then Earl of Galloway, who established it in the late 18thC.

DETOURS: Twelve miles northwest of Newton Stewart on the A 712 is Clatteringshaws Loch, site of Clatteringshaws Wildlife Centre (1000-1700 April-Oct.), which features local history displays, and Bruce's Stone, which commemorates the Battle of Rapploch Moss in 1307, one of Robert the Bruce's (see **A-Z**) successful skirmishes against the

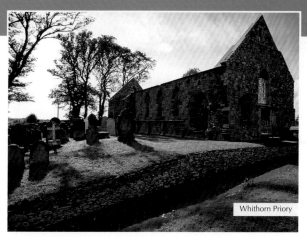

Whithorn Priory

English. Alternatively, you could take the A 714 north for 10 miles to Glentrool Village and Loch Trool, from where there are wide views over the desolate landscape. On a bluff above the loch stands the Bruce Stone, indicating the site of another skirmish in 1306, during which Robert the Bruce and his men rolled boulders onto their hapless foe. A memorial tomb to six Covenanters (see **A-Z**), killed while at prayer, stands nearby. Join the A 714 and head south.

106 miles – Wigtown. The Museum (1400-1600 Mon., Wed. & Fri., May-Sep.) tells the story of the Wigtown Martyrs, two women who were drowned on stakes in the bay in 1685 for refusing to renounce their Covenanting beliefs. They are buried in the churchyard. Head south out of town on the A 714, then take the A 746.

117 miles – Whithorn. St. Ninian's (see **A-Z**) original AD 397 white house was built here. It has been excavated but has had to be re-covered to preserve it. Whithorn Priory was founded in 1160 as a shrine and place of pilgrimage. The adjacent museum explains the history while at the Whithorn Dig (1030-1700; £1.25, child 50p, family £3) you can see the continuing archaeological excavation of the site. Go south again on the A 750.

120 miles – Isle of Whithorn. An attractive village set round a small harbour. Visit St. Ninian's Chapel which is associated with early

Christian development in Scotland. Take the A 750 back for half a mile, then turn onto the A 747.

DETOUR: After 2 miles turn left for St. Ninian's Cave. The car park is a mile off the main road, and from here it is a walk of 1.5 miles through the woods to the cove which was St. Ninian's retreat. Note the early Christian crosses carved into the rock. Retrace your route back to the main road and continue through Glasserton and Monreith.

129 miles – Barsalloch Fort. On the right-hand side is this Iron-Age hillfort. The A 747 follows the craggy coastline through Port William until its junction with the A 75. Turn left then right into Glenluce. Follow a narrow road beneath the old viaduct and signs for the abbey, 1.5 miles away. Glenluce Abbey (0930-1900 Mon.-Sat., 1400-1900 Sun.; 60p, child 30p) was founded in 1192 by Cistercian monks. The 15thC chapterhouse remains partially intact. Note the unusual red-clay water pipes. Rejoin the A 75 and continue west.

149 miles – Castle Kennedy Gardens (1000-1700 April-Sep.; £1, child 50p, no dogs). These gardens, set around the Black and White lochs, with the castle ruins on an isthmus, are fabulous. Attractions include the lily pond, monkey puzzle trees, azaleas, magnolias and 35 species of rhododendrons. Take the road west.

154 miles– Stranraer. Pop: 10,000. Full services. Tourist Information (Easter-Oct.), Port Rodie Car Park, tel: 0776-2595. On the shores of Loch Ryan, this is the car ferry port to Northern Ireland. The Wigtown District Museum (1000-1700 Mon.-Sat.; free) in London Rd has displays on dairy farming and Sir John Ross, the Arctic explorer (1777-1856), whose house, now the Northwest Castle Hotel, can be seen opposite the pier.

DETOUR: The double-ended peninsula in the southwest corner of Scotland is known as the Rhins of Galloway. Seven miles southwest of Stranraer on the A 77 stands Portpatrick, now a small holiday resort but between 1661 and 1849 the departure point for sailings to Northern

Logan Botanic Gardens

Ireland. However, with the advent of steam, all sailings transferred to Stranraer. Dunskey Castle, built in the 15thC and now in ruins, stands on nearby cliffs. Continue on the B 7042 and A 716 to Ardwell House Gardens (1000-1800, walled garden till 1700, Easter-Oct.; £1, child 50p), with their daffodils and rhododendrons, then on the B 7065 to Logan Botanic Gardens (1000-1800 Mar.-Oct.; £1.50, child £1). This area is fortunate in having the mildest climate in Scotland, and many subtropical plants, such as palms and tree-ferns, flourish here. On the north shore of Logan Bay is a Fish Pond, built into the rock in 1800 to serve as a larder for nearby Logan House but now containing fish which can be fed by hand. The Mull of Galloway, the most southerly point in Scotland, with its lighthouse and 200 ft cliffs, is a further 7 miles south. Return to Stranraer on the A 716.

Turn north out of town on the A 77. The road hugs the loch shore for several miles before turning inland.

169 miles – Ballantrae. On the hill above this pretty village lies the hamlet of Garleffin with its semicircle of seven standing stones, of Druid origin, opposite the houses. Continue north on the A 77, following the rocky coastline.

181 miles – Girvan. Pop: 8000. Full services. Tourist Information (April-Oct.), Bridge St, tel: 0465-4950. An old smuggling town which, with its harbour and beaches, is popular in summer. On nearby Dowhill are the remains of a Pictish (see **Picts**) fort. Return to the main road and drive north. Along this coast there are excellent views of Ailsa Craig, the 114 ft-high granite rock 10 miles offshore, a bird sanctuary with colonies of gannets and guillemots. It can be reached from Girvan by boat. For permission contact the Marquis of Ailsa, tel: 06556-646. After 4.5 miles turn left onto the A 719.

186 miles – Turnberry. Famed for its links golf course and plush hotel. Also see the ruins of Turnberry Castle where Robert the Bruce spent his childhood. Passing through Maidens, look out for the turn-off to the right to Kirkoswald which is 1.5 miles off the A 719. This is the site of Souter Johnnie's Cottage, the thatched home of souter (cobbler) John Davidson who was immortalized in Robert Burns' poem *Tam o' Shanter*. Rejoin the A 719 and continue north.

191 miles – Culzean Castle & Country Park (castle 1000-1800, park 0900-sunset, April-Sep.; park £3 per car, castle £2.10 extra, child £1.05). Tourist Information (April-Sep.), tel: 06556-293. Designed by Robert Adam (see **A-Z**) for the Earl of Cassillis (1772-92), the castle is sited on a cliff top which affords wonderful views of the Firth of Clyde. Inside it is beautifully furnished with its round drawing room and oval staircase. The Eisenhower exhibition details the General and later US President's role as Commander in Chief of Allied Forces in Europe during World War II, the connection with him being that after victory he was granted a suite of rooms in the castle for the rest of his life. There are 565 acres of grounds, including an aviary, walled garden, deer park, walks and tearoom. Return to the main road.

Alloway

194 miles – The Electric Brae. An optical illusion created by the geography of the surrounding hills which makes the road appear to go up when in fact it's going down! Continue on the A 719.

197 miles – Dunure. The village, reached by turning left off the main road, is overlooked by the ruins of Dunure Castle. In the castle's back vault the Earl of Cassillis is said to have roasted alive the abbot of Crossraguel Abbey to force him to give up the abbey lands! Rejoin the A 719 and continue north, past the cliffs known as the Heads of Ayr. Turn right off the A 719.

201 miles – Alloway. Burns' Cottage and Museum (0900-1900 June-Aug., 1000-1700 Sep.-May; £1.50, child 75p) is where the poet was born. Five hundred yards to the right of the junction is the Burns Monument and Garden containing the Land o'Burns Centre with its audio-visual presentation about his life. Nearby is the Auld Brig o'Doon, the arched bridge that features in *Tam o'Shanter*. Continue along Alloway Pl. towards Ayr.

203 miles – Ayr (see **A-Z**). Leave the town, following the signs for the A 77. From Fenwick Moor, beyond Kilmarnock, there are fine views across the Firth of Clyde to Arran (see **A-Z**). The A 72 joins the M 8 to take you into Glasgow (see **A-Z**) (238 miles).

Auld Brig o'Doon

Dumfries

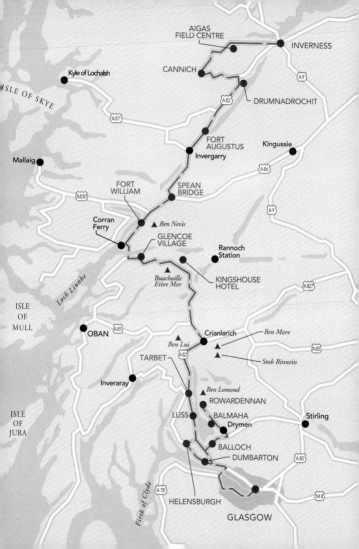

AIGAS
FIELD CENTRE

INVERNESS

CANNICH

Kyle of Lochalsh

ISLE OF SKYE

DRUMNADROCHIT

A82

A9

A87

FORT
AUGUSTUS

Kingussie

Invergarry

Mallaig

A86

A830

SPEAN
BRIDGE

A9

FORT
WILLIAM

Corran
Ferry

▲ Ben Nevis

GLENCOE
VILLAGE

Rannoch
Station

Buachaille
Etive Mor

A827

KINGSHOUSE
HOTEL

Loch Linnhe

ISLE
OF
MULL

OBAN

A85

Crianlarich

Ben More

▲

Ben Lui

▲

A82

▲

Stob Binnein

TARBET

A85

Inveraray

▲ Ben Lomond

ROWARDENNAN

ISLE
OF
JURA

LUSS

BALMAHA

Stirling

Drymen

BALLOCH

A80

DUMBARTON

A78

HELENSBURGH

M8

GLASGOW

Firth of Clyde

Loch Lomond & Glencoe

Glasgow–Inverness. Duration: 3 days.

From Glasgow take the M 8 west, exit at Junction 30 and cross the
Erskine Bridge (toll 40p), built in 1971 and spanning the River Clyde.
Turn left on the A 82. There is a lovely view down the river from here,
with the Renfrew Hills rising above the opposite bank.

20 miles – Dumbarton. Pop: 23,000. Full services. In this ancient
county town turn left on Victoria St to reach Dumbarton Castle (HS site,
see **Opening Times**, but closed 1230-1330; 60p, child 30p), spectacularly situated atop a steep, rocky crag. It was from here in 1548 that the
infant Mary, Queen of Scots (see **A-Z**) was sent to France to be married
to the French dauphin. In the town centre, beside the car park in Castle
St, is the Denny Ship Model Experiment Tank, part of the Scottish
Maritime Museum (1000-1600 Mon.-Sat.; 50p, child 25p). You can
take a guided tour of the testing facility where the design of thousands
of ships, including that of the *Queen Mary*, was perfected. Continue on
the A 82 then turn right on the A 811.

DETOUR: Follow the A 814 to Helensburgh, where you can visit The Hill
House (1300-1700; £1.90, child 95p) on Upper Colquhoun St, which
was designed by Charles Rennie Mackintosh (see **A-Z**). Completed in
1904, this distinctive house is a superb example of Mackintosh's work.
Take the B 832 and B 881 from Helensburgh to rejoin the A 82 at
Arden and turn right.

27 miles – Balloch. Full services. Tourist Information (April-Oct.),
Balloch Rd, tel: 0389-53533. A popular weekend resort at the south-
ernmost tip of Loch Lomond. By the bridge over the River Leven (daily
cruises on the loch from Sweeney's Cruises, 1 hr £2.50, 2 hr £3.50;
Balloch to Luss £3.50; rowing boats £2.50 per hr, £12 per day), a minor
road leads to Balloch Pier. A pleasant picnic area with views up the
loch to Ben Lomond overlooks the pier where the vintage paddle
steamer *Maid of the Loch* lies rusting. Nearby, the traditional cruise
boat *Countess Fiona* lies hauled out on the slipway. Cruises have been
suspended temporarily while the boats await a buyer. Just to the east of
the town is Balloch Castle Country Park (0800-sunset; free), with
lochside walks in beautiful ornamental grounds. Follow the A 811 east
for 8 miles, then turn left on the B 837 at Drymen (continue straight on

Deerstalking above Loch Lomond

here to join **EXCURSION 3** at Stirling), passing through Buchanan Smithy, with an interesting workshop in the middle of a row of houses on the right – 'David Smith, maker of fine swords for gentlemen' – where you can watch a master smith at work (1000-1700; free). Balmaha is a small village on a pretty, wooded bay on Loch Lomond, with a restaurant, chip shop, petrol station, boat hire and loch cruises. The lochside road continues another 6 miles past forest walks and picnic sites to Rowardennan, where there are a large hotel, youth hostel and passenger ferry to Inverbeg (see below). From Rowardennan you can climb a well-marked path for 3.5 miles to the summit of Ben Lomond (3192 ft) (see **Walking**). Return to the A 82 and head north. The road along Loch Lomond-side is a popular holiday route and can be very busy in July and Aug., and on summer weekends. The scenery is impressive, with the loch narrowing and the surrounding mountains getting higher as you go north. Passing Cameron Wildlife Park, Duck Bay Marina and the ornamental gateway to Rossdht House, seat of the Colquhoun family (closed to the public), you reach the pretty lochside village of Luss. There is a hotel and tearoom, and loch cruises from the pier (30 min cruise on *Lomond Lady*; £2). Beyond Luss, the loch narrows and the bulk of Ben Lomond rises majestically on your right. At Inverbeg there are a hotel and youth hostel, and a passenger ferry across the loch to Rowardennan (see above).

44 miles – Tarbet. Limited
services. Tourist Information (April-Oct.), Pier Rd,
tel: 03012-260. (Turn left
here to Arrochar to start
EXCURSION 4A.) Turn right
on the A 82 to Crianlarich.
The road on this stretch of

PEACE WITH THE COMING AND THE PARTING GUEST

the loch is narrower and more twisting, but passes through lovely natu-
ral woods which are thickly carpeted with Scottish bluebells in May
and June. Beyond the head of the loch, the road climbs up Glen
Falloch (parking area beside the Falls of Falloch, 2 miles past
Inverarnan), through the village of Crianlarich. About 2 miles before
Tyndrum you should stop to admire the grand mountain scenery;
shapely Ben Lui off to the left of the road, and the twin conical peaks of
Ben More and Stob Binnein back in the direction of Crianlarich.

65 miles – Tyndrum. Limited services. Tourist Information (Mar.-Oct.),
tel: 08304-246. Continuing on the A 82, the road ascends to Bridge of
Orchy Hotel, beyond which there are good views to the popular hill-
walking area called the Black Mount, with the waters of Loch Tulla in
the foreground. The views improve as the road winds up the hillside
beyond the loch, and brings you to the desolate expanse of Rannoch
Moor, a vast basin of peat dotted with countless lochans, which stretches all the way to Rannoch station in the east (see **EXCURSION 11**). The
maze of interconnecting waterways between the lochans has encour-
aged various intrepid adventurers to swim, canoe or skate across the
moor! At the summit, the road sweeps round to the left and suddenly
you are confronted with a wonderful view of the peaks that guard the
entrance to fabled Glencoe, notably the pyramid-shaped Buachaille
Etive Mor (The Great Herdsman of Etive) (3345 ft). A minor road on the
left leads to the White Corries Chairlift (1000-1700 summer), and to the
right is the Kingshouse Hotel, Scotland's oldest inn, which offers
accommodation, bar meals and mountain bike hire. Just beyond the
bridge on the main road is a minor road on the left, giving a 14 mile
scenic drive down beautiful Glen Etive. As the main road reaches its
highest point after passing beneath the rock climbers' playground of the

Buachaille, you get your first view down Glencoe, with the brooding crags of The Three Sisters rising on the left, and the steep mountain wall of Aonach Eagach on the right. Descend into the upper gorge of the River Coe, past a splendid waterfall on the left, to reach a white farmhouse at the Meeting of the Three Waters. A few hundred yards further on there is a large layby on the left.

WALK: 2 hr. From the layby there is an interesting walk to the Lost Valley, a hidden mountain meadow tucked between the first and second of The Three Sisters. The path descends to the east of the layby, towards a footbridge over the river, then climbs by the little stream that falls from the valley, mostly invisible beneath boulders. The path passes between huge rocks amid beautiful birch woods, and finally debouches onto the flat meadow, where cattle-raiders once concealed their ill-gotten herds. Retrace your route to the layby.

Continue down the glen past Loch Achtriochtan and take the minor road on the right to the Clachaig Inn, a traditional climbers' pub and hotel with live folk music on Sat. night, close to the site of the infamous Glencoe Massacre (see **A-Z**). There are forest walks behind the hotel, and a footbridge across the river leads to the NTS Visitor Centre (1000-1730 April, May & Oct., 0930-1830 June-Sep.), also accessible by car from the main road. The road continues beyond Clachaig to Glencoe Village. Turn left.

98 miles – Ballachulish. Limited services. Tourist Information (April-Oct.), tel: 08552-296. The village is surrounded by a number of old slate quarries. Take the A 82 at the roundabout and go over Ballachulish Bridge, from where there is a good view back up Loch Leven, with the prominent peak of the Pap of Glencoe. Beyond Onich the road follows the shore of Loch Linnhe, passing Corran Ferry (cars and passengers to Ardgour).

112 miles – Fort William (see **A-Z**). Take the A 82 north. At the edge of the town is a roundabout with a minor road right to Glen Nevis, a beautiful 9 mile drive round the west and south sides of Ben Nevis (see **A-Z**). After one mile is a parking area at the foot of a path up the mountain, the highest in the British Isles. The road continues past a caravan/camp site, the excellent Glen Nevis Restaurant and Bar, and the youth hostel, crosses the river at a waterfall and passes under Polldubh Crags, popular with rock climbers, before ending at a parking area by a huge waterslide.

WALK: 1.5 hr. Follow the path at the end of the parking area. The route is easy to follow but stony, so stout footwear is recommended. It follows the north bank of the River Nevis as it roars through a rocky, wooded gorge for half a mile then emerges unexpectedly in a lovely green meadow ringed by mountains, with the spectacular Steall Waterfall on the hillside opposite. For those with a steady head, there is

an Indiana Jones-style wire bridge across the river to a mountaineers' bothy and beyond to the south side of the waterfall, from where there is a good view of the back of Ben Nevis. Return to the parking area by the same path.

Back on the A 82, 2 miles out of Fort William a minor road on the left leads to the imposing ruins of the late 13thC Inverlochy Castle (temporarily closed for repairs). Turn left on the A 830 (continue straight on here for the Aonach Mor Gondola – see **Fort William**), crossing the Caledonian Canal at Neptune's Staircase, the steep flight of locks marking the entrance to this waterway, completed in 1882 and linking Loch Linnhe with the Moray Firth at Inverness. Just after the canal, turn right at Banavie on the B 8004. This road offers spectacular views of the craggy north face of Ben Nevis, which often holds snow patches all through the summer, and rejoins the A 82 at the famous Commando Memorial near Spean Bridge, erected in 1952 in memory of the World War II soldiers who trained in this area. (Turn right here to reach the A 86 which joins **EXCURSION 11** at Kingussie.) Continue to the left on the A 82 along the banks of Loch Lochy, perhaps stopping for tea and scones in the tearoom beside Laggan Locks. A few miles further on, at a car park opposite a shop, is the Well of the Seven Heads, marked by a spire topped with a sculpture of seven severed heads. This gruesome 19thC monument records a notorious 17thC murder, described on the monument in English, Gaelic, Latin and French. The spring itself is in a low tunnel under the monument. Continue north along Loch Oich-side through Invergarry. (Turn left here on the A 87 past lochs Garry and Cluanie, and through scenic Glen Shiel to reach the west coast at Kintail and the Skye ferry at Kyle of Lochalsh – see **EXCURSION 6**.)

141 miles – Fort Augustus. Pop: 1000. Full services. Tourist Information (April-mid Oct.), Car Park, tel: 0320-6367. A pretty town set at the southern tip of Loch Ness. There are pleasant walks to be enjoyed along the towpath of the Caledonian Canal, and in Auchterawe (turn left just beyond the town: information on walks available from the Forestry Commission office). Between the town and the loch is Fort Augustus Abbey School, built on and around the 18thC fort built by Gen. Wade (see **A-Z**) that gives the town its name (tours by arrangement, tel: 0320-62344; but the church is always open). The road now follows the shores of Loch Ness, famous for its elusive monster. The greatest number of sightings have been made from Urquhart Castle (HS site, see **Opening Times**, but 0930-1900 Sun., April-Sep.; £1, child 50p), an impressive ruin 18 miles north of Fort Augustus.

160 miles – Drumnadrochit. This village contains two exhibitions dedicated to Loch Ness and its monster. Cross the bridge, turn left on the A 831, and immediately on the right is the Loch Ness Visitor Centre (0900-1800; £2, child £1), which offers an interesting 20 min film on the search for the monster, but little else save poster displays, a coffee house and a souvenir shop. A better bet is the official Loch Ness Monster Exhibition Centre (0900-1915; £2.75, child £1.50) on the A 82. A visit will take about 1 hr. The presentation covers the story of the monster from the roots of the story in local legend to the present-day high-tech exploration of the loch, and includes tableaux, videos, music, photographs, taped commentary and displays of the actual equipment used in the monster hunt. From Drumnadrochit, take the A 831 towards Cannich. A few miles before Cannich, a track on the left (signposted) leads to Corrimony Cairn, a large neolithic burial cairn surrounded by a ring of standing stones.

172 miles – Cannich. From here a minor road leads west for 10 miles along beautiful Glen Affric, past many tempting picnic spots. At the end of the road is a car park with a notice board describing a number of good walks. WALK: 3-4 hr. From the car park take the track along the north bank of Loch Affric (muddy in places), returning along the Land Rover track on the south bank of the loch. The head of the loch is set amid grand mountain scenery (hill-walking gear, map and compass recommended). Keen walkers can continue west from the head of the loch to reach remote Alltbeithe Youth Hostel, and from there to the west coast at Kintail (see **EXCURSION 5**), about 20 miles from the car park.

From Cannich the A 831 descends attractive Strathglass, lined with lovely bluebell woods in early summer. A few miles beyond Struy is the Aigas Field Centre (0900-1800, tel: 0463-782443), which offers daily expeditions into the surrounding hills to observe local wildlife. There are also nature trails, angling and a shop. On reaching the A 862, turn right to reach the shores of the Beauly Firth and, a few miles later, the highland capital of Inverness (see **A-Z**) (190 miles).

Fort Augustus

Bannockburn Monument

Ardnamurchan Lighthouse

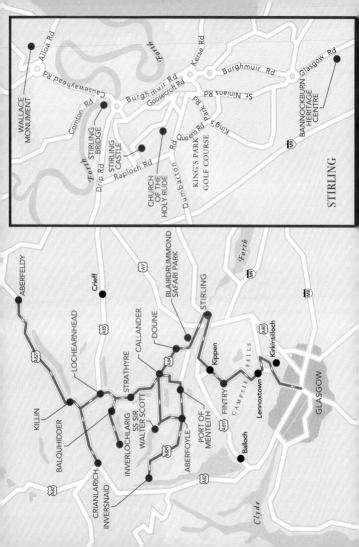

STIRLING

WALLACE MONUMENT

Alloa Rd

Forth

Causewayhead Rd

Corton Rd

Burgh muir Rd

Goosecroft Rd

Kerse Rd

Burghmuir Rd

Glasgow Rd

St. Ninians Rd

BANNOCKBURN HERITAGE CENTRE

(M9)

STIRLING BRIDGE

Drip Rd

Forth

STIRLING CASTLE

Raploch Rd

Dumbarton Rd

Queens Rd

King's Park Rd

KING'S PARK GOLF COURSE

CHURCH OF THE HOLY RUDE

ABERFELDY

(A827)

Crieff

(A9)

(A85)

BLAIRDRUMMOND SAFARI PARK

Forth

KILLIN

BALQUHIDDER

LOCHEARNHEAD

STRATHYRE

CALLANDER

DOUNE

STIRLING

(M9)

(M80)

(M8)

CRIANLARICH

INVERSNAID

INVERLOCHLARIG

SS SIR WALTER SCOTT

(B829)

PORT OF MENTEITH

ABERFOYLE

(A81)

Kippen

FINTRY

CAMPSIE FELLS

Lennoxtown

Kirkintilloch

(A80)

(A803)

GLASGOW

Balloch

(A82)

Clyde

The Trossachs

Glasgow–Aberfeldy/Crianlarich. Duration: 2 days.

Take the M 8 east out of Glasgow. At Junction 15, follow the A 803 signposted Kirkintilloch and continue through Bishopbriggs. A couple of miles beyond on the left-hand side beside the towpath of the Forth and Clyde Canal, is the Stables Inn. The canal, when built in 1790, provided a waterborne link between east and west Scotland. The MS *Ferry Queen* carries passengers to Bishopbriggs and there are pleasant walks along the towpath. Continue on the A 803 through Kirkintilloch then turn left onto the A 891. At Milton of Campsie the road runs along the foot of the Campsie Fells. Continue for 2 miles, enter Lennoxtown, turn right onto the B 822 and begin the steep climb into the Campsies. There are excellent views up and down the valley and also good, if windswept, walking. Magnificent views appear to the north and west into the Trossachs as the road switchbacks down off the barren tops and into the Endrick Valley.

21 miles – Fintry. An attractive old village enveloped by the surrounding hills. In the centre of the village turn right onto the B 822 signposted Kippen. Culcreuch Castle Hotel on the right after 1 mile dates back to 1296 and was the clan castle of the Galbraiths for three centuries. Set in a 1600 acre estate it's an idyllic place to stay or just to have lunch. Continue on the B 822 to Kippen. Turn right onto the A 811.

38 miles – Stirling (see **A-Z**). From Stirling follow the A 84. After 3 miles is the Blairdrummond Safari Park (1000-1730, last entry 1630, Easter-Sep.; £4.50, child £3). Attractions include lions, elephants, giraffes, camels, performing seals, leisure facilities and waterslides. A safari bus is available for those without private transport.

44 miles – Doune. On approaching the village you cross a bridge over the River Teith which was built by James IV's tailor to spite the ferryman who had denied him passage. A 'must' is the well-preserved late-14thC castle (0930-1900 Mon.-Sat., 1400-1900 Sun.; £1, child 50p), protected by two rivers and a moat, which is striking both inside and out. It served as a dower house for three Scottish queens and later as a prison. Rejoin the A 84. After one mile is the Doune Motor Museum (1000-1700; £1.80, child 90p), a fine collection of vintage and more modern cars, including Jaguars, Lagondas and the second-oldest Rolls Royce in

the world. Continue along the A 84 through an attractive valley with Ben Ledi visible ahead in the distance.

51 miles – Callander. Pop: 2500. Full services. The capital of the Trossachs and the 'Tannochbrae' of television's *Dr Finlay's Casebook*. Well worth a visit is the Rob Roy Visitor Centre (and Tourist Information office) in old St. Kessog's Church which tells this legendary character's story (see **Rob Roy**) (1000-1700 Mar.-May, 1000-1800 June & Sep., 0930-1930 July & Aug.; £1.65, child £1.25). Turn left in the town centre onto the A 81 signposted Glasgow. After 5 miles there is a brilliant view down to the Lake of Menteith, the only lake in Scotland. At the intersection with the A 873 turn right and continue on the A 81.

57 miles – Port of Menteith. Turn left to the attractive parish church on the lakeshore. Half a mile beyond the church is the car park and ferry for Inchmahome Priory (0930-1900 Mon.-Sat., 1400-1900 Sun., April-Sep.; ferry £1, child 50p). This Augustinian priory, built by the Earl of Menteith in 1238, sits on an island. The infant Mary, Queen of Scots (see **A-Z**) was sheltered here after the Scots' defeat at the Battle of Pinkie, before being sent on to France. Rejoin the A 81 and turn right at the T-junction.

62 miles – Aberfoyle. Pop: 600. Full services. Tourist Information (April-Oct.), Main St, tel: 08772-352.

DETOUR: Take the narrow B 829 for 11 miles to Stronachlachar on the banks of Loch Katrine and further round, past Loch Arklet, to Inversnaid on the remote eastern shore of Loch Lomond. There's a secluded hotel, with Ben Lomond standing just to the south. Glengyle, where Rob Roy had his family home, lies a little to the north of Stronachlachar.

Leave Aberfoyle on the A 821 which climbs steeply up to the Dukes Pass. After one mile the David Marshall Lodge and Visitor Centre (1000-1800; 10p per car) on the right is a scenic viewpoint looking south to the Campsie Fells and west to Ben Lomond. Many walks into the Queen Elizabeth Forest Park begin here too. On the other side of the pass there is a panoramic view into the Trossachs and across to Perthshire, making it a wonderful place to picnic. The A 821 now descends into the long glen ribboned by glittering lochs and surrounded by tree-covered craggy peaks which is known as the Trossachs. It forms the setting for two of Sir Walter Scott's (see **A-Z**) works, *The Lady*

of the Lake and *Rob Roy*. The
A 821 skirts the southern edge of
Loch Achray then splits. Take the
turn-off to the left through a narrow wooded gorge to the eastern
tip of Loch Katrine.

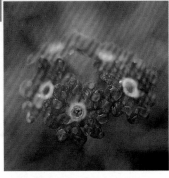

70 miles – Loch Katrine. Sailings
on the old steamer SS *Sir Walter
Scott* to Stronachlachar at the
western end of the loch run May-
Sep. (1100, 1345 & 1515 Mon.-
Fri., 1400 & 1530 Sat. & Sun.), enabling you to see Loch Katrine and
the Trossachs at their best. Rob Roy and his clan would hide the cattle
they stole on nearby Ellen's Isle. For those with an aversion to water
there's a road along the northern shore of the loch to Glengyle and
Stronachlachar (see page 59). Ben Venue (2393 ft) sits at the southeast-
ern end of the loch. Return along the A 821 as it hugs the northern
shore of Loch Achray.

72 miles – The Trossachs Hotel. This striking hotel with its twin round
towers and conical spires is open to non-residents. A broad tree-lined
valley separates Loch Achray from Loch Venachar, at the head of which
stands Brig o'Turk. Open fields line the northern shore of the loch as
the valley widens, giving easy access to the waterfront. At the eastern
end of the loch the road drops down towards the hollow in which
Callander nestles. Five and a half miles beyond Brig o'Turk the A 821
joins the A 84. Turn left following signs for Crianlarich and up through
the narrow Pass of Leny.

79 miles – The Falls of Leny. A footpath leads from a car park on the
right through dense conifers to this attractive waterfall. Shortly after the
road joins the southerly tip of Loch Lubnaig ('bent loch'), the steep
sides of Ben Ledi (2873 ft) tumbling into its stunningly beautiful waters.
Rugged mountains envelop this fairy-tale valley on all sides. Continue
for 4 miles to Strathyre Forest Information Centre (0930-1900). The forest was established in the 1930s and now incorporates over eight million trees, filling the valley. The centre examines forest management
and has details of trails and walks.

Loch Earn

85 miles – Strathyre. Wordsworth stayed here in 1803 and this single-street village remains a good centre for exploring the Trossachs.
DETOUR: At the Kingshouse Hotel turn left to Balquhidder, 2 miles away. Rob Roy is buried with his wife and sons in the graveyard of Balquhidder Parish Church. A fitting epitaph, 'MacGregor Despite Them', is inscribed above the grave. The village itself stands on the eastern shore of Loch Voil. Stronvar House Hotel, in a romantic setting half a mile away on the lochside, was built in 1825 and was first a family home, then a youth hostel in the 1960s and is now a pleasant hotel. A narrow road follows along the northern shore of Loch Voil for 6.5 miles to Inverlochlarig, where Rob Roy spent the final years of his life. There are many fine stopping places on this road where you could swim and have picnics. At Inverlochlarig there's a Tourist Information board with a map showing walks into the surrounding mountains. Return to the A 84 and turn left.
92 miles – Lochearnhead. This spacious village stands beside Loch Earn. There are numerous hotels and B&Bs, and water-sports facilities. Follow the A 85 north through Glen Ogle for 5 miles to Glen Dochart. A right turn will take you on the A 827 through Killin, where you will see the dramatic Falls of Dochart, and alongside Loch Tay to Aberfeldy (see **EXCURSION 11**), or you can continue on the A 85 to Crianlarich (see **EXCURSION 2**) (11 miles) or Oban (see **EXCURSIONS 4B & 5**) (49 miles).

Loch Lomond

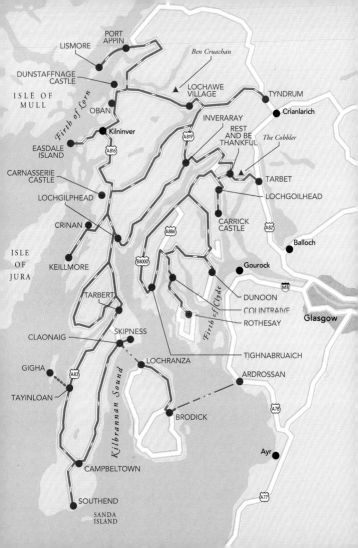

Tarbet/Tyndrum–Lochgilphead, Lochgilphead–Campbeltown.
Duration: 2–3 days.

This route leaves **EXCURSION 2** at either Tarbet (**EXCURSION 4A**) or
Tyndrum (**EXCURSION 4B**).

Excursion 4A:
At Tarbet on Loch Lomond-side, bear left on the A 83 for Lochgilphead
to reach the village of Arrochar. On a clear day there is a good view
across the loch to the jagged, rocky peak called The Cobbler (2891 ft).
The road rounds the head of Loch Long, then bends sharp right to begin
the long climb up Glen Croe to the pass known as the Rest and be
Thankful, at 807 ft.
DETOUR: 2 day, 130 mile trip to the Cowal Peninsula. At the summit of
the pass, turn left on the B 828, dropping steeply down Glen More.
Lochgoilhead. A centre for water sports and forest walks. In town is the
Drimsynie Leisure Complex, tel: 03013-247/3444, where you will find
the European Sheep and Wool Centre (shows 1100, 1300 & 1500
Mon.-Fri.; £2, child £1), which offers displays of sheep-shearing, work-
ing sheepdogs and 19 different breeds of sheep. On the west shore of
Loch Goil, a few miles south of the town, is the romantic ruin of 15thC
Carrick Castle. Head north again, and fork left on the B 839, which
climbs up the twisting Hell's Glen to a grand view across the upper
reaches of Loch Fyne towards Ben Cruachan. At the foot of the hill, go
left on the A 815 along the wooded shores of Loch Fyne, turn right at
Creggans on the A 886, then right again after a few miles on the
B 8000. This pleasant minor road follows the quiet east shore of the
loch down to Ardlamont Point, then turns north along the Kyles of Bute
to Tighnabruaich, a small resort which comes complete with tearooms
and B&Bs. Take the A 8003 north. A few miles beyond the village is
a picnic area on the right, from where there are beautiful views over the
Kyles of Bute, the narrow strait that separates the island of Bute from
the mainland. To visit the island, drive around the head of Loch Riddon
to Colintraive, where there is a regular ferry service (crossing time 5
min; car £4.10, passenger 50p). The island is a popular, though rather
old-fashioned, summer resort.

Rothesay. Pop: 5500. Full services. Tourist Information (all year), The Pier, tel: 0700-2151. The island's main town, where the major attraction (apart from the prom with its amusement arcades, crazy golf and funfair) is Rothesay Castle (HS site, see **Opening Times**; 80p, child 40p), an important 12th-13thC stronghold, unique in Scotland in being circular in plan. Behind the castle is the Museum (1030-1630 April-Sep., 1430-1630 Oct.-Mar.; 70p, child 35p), and on the High St, towards the edge of town, is the Leisure Pool (1200-2100 Mon.-Fri., 1200-1700 Sat., 1400-1700 Sun.; 90p, child 55p). The rest of the island offers pleasant picnicking and walking, and some mediocre beaches. A car ferry service connects Rothesay with Wemyss Bay, only 33 miles from Glasgow city centre.

Back on the mainland, 5 miles north of Colintraive, the B 836 leads east to Holy Loch, where you turn right on the A 815.

Dunoon. Pop: 10,000. Full services. Tourist Information (all year), 7 Alexandra Parade, tel: 0369-3785. This is the principal town of the Cowal Peninsula, and a busy resort, but there is little to see, save for the famous statue of Highland Mary, a sweetheart of Robert Burns (see **A-Z**), and the Cowal Highland Gathering (see **Events**). Regular car ferries ply to Gourock, 30 miles from Glasgow. The A 815 leads north from Dunoon, passing the beautiful Younger Botanic Garden (1000-1800 April-Oct.; 60p, child 30p) and long, narrow Loch Eck, to return to Loch Fyne at Strachur. Turn right here to rejoin the main excursion at Glen Kinglass.

From the Rest and be Thankful, the road sweeps down through Glen Kinglas and round the head of Loch Fyne, passing Strone House Gardens (0900-2100 April-Oct.; £1, child free), which contain Britain's tallest tree.

Inveraray Jail

24 miles – Inveraray. Pop: 1000.
Tourist Information (Easter-Sep.),
Front St, tel: 0499-2063. An
attractive 18thC town on the
lochside near the fairy-tale towers
of Inveraray Castle, seat of the
Campbell family, dukes of Argyll.
The Castle (1000-1300, 1400-
1730 Mon.-Thu. & Sat., 1400-

1730 Sun., April & May, Sep. & Oct.; 1000-1730 Mon.-Sat., 1400-1730
Sun., June-Aug.; £2.50, child £1.50), built 1740-90 to replace the original 15thC structure (now ruined), houses a fine collection of 18thC furniture, weapons, tapestries and paintings, while the town is a rare
example of 18thC town-planning. On the left of the church at the top of
Main St is the old Inveraray Jail (0930-1800; £2.45, child £1.10, family
£6), now an interesting museum telling the story of crime and punish-
ment in Scotland from the 16th-19thC. The route continues south along
Loch Fyne, passing Auchindrain Township (1100-1600 Sun.-Fri., April,
May & Sep., 1000-1700 June-Aug.; £2, child £1.20, family £5.50), a
living museum of West Highland farming life, and Crarae Glen Garden
(0900-1800; £2, child 70p), famed for its beautiful rhododendrons and
azaleas, to arrive at Lochgilphead (see page 72).

Excursion 4B:

At Tyndrum, fork left on the A 85 to Dalmally and the north end of the scenic, 23 mile long Loch Awe.

DETOURS: Here the A 819 leads south to Inveraray (see **EXCURSION 4A**), and after 6 miles the B 840 forks right and hugs the shores of fresh-water Loch Awe, offering pleasant walking, picnicking and fishing. It rejoins **EXCURSION 4B** after 24 miles at Carnasserie Castle (see page 71). The head of Loch Awe is commanded by the romantic ruin of 15thC Kilchurn Castle (no access to interior), beyond which is the little village of Lochawe. Turn steeply down to the left to a car park by the railway, and walk over the bridge to Lochawe Pier, from where you can take a cruise on the Edwardian steamlaunch *Lady Rowena* (1030-1700 June-Sep., Sat. & Sun. only in May; £1-5.50, child 50p-£2.75) or enjoy tea and cakes in the unusual setting of a restored pullman car that used to run on the neighbouring West Highland line. Beyond Lochawe, both road and railway are channelled into the narrow defile of the Pass of Brander, Loch Awe's outlet to the sea, and the site of a bloody battle in 1308. Here you will find the Cruachan Power Station Visitors' Centre

(0900-1630 Easter-Oct.; £1.25, child 50p), where you can join a 20 min tour of the 400,000 kW hydro-electric power station housed in a huge cavern in the hillside. Five miles further on, at Taynuilt, a road on the right leads to Bonawe Iron Furnace (HS site, see **Opening Times**, but closed Oct.-Mar.; £1, child 50p), near the shore of Loch Etive. This major smelting works was in operation from 1753 until 1874, and among other things produced cannon and cannonballs for the Royal Navy. It has been beautifully restored. From nearby Bonawe Pier there are daily 3 hr cruises up Loch Etive (1400, also 1030 May-Sep.; £4.50, child £2.50). The main road continues to the mouth of Loch Etive at Connel Bridge. The rocky narrows here constrict the tidal flow in and out of the 20 mile-long loch, causing the spectacular rapids known as the Falls of Lora, which are at their best during the few hours either side of low water.

DETOUR: The A 828 goes north across the bridge and leads in 32 miles to Ballachulish (see **EXCURSION 2**). Attractions on this road include the sandy beach of Benderloch, just beyond the bridge; the Oban Sea Life Centre (0900-1800 Feb.-June, Sep.-Nov., 0900-1900 July & Aug.; £2.95, child £1.95), a large aquarium displaying the underwater life of Scotland's west coast, including a chance to see seals close to; pretty Port Appin, where there is a passenger ferry to the lovely island of Lismore; and 16thC Castle Stalker, picturesquely set on an islet near the shore (visits by arrangement only, tel: 0883-2768).

A few miles beyond Connel Bridge, on the right, you will see 13thC Dunstaffnage Castle (HS site, see **Opening Times**; 60p, child 30p), before the road finally drops down to Oban.

37 miles – Oban (see **EXCURSION 5, A-Z**). From Oban, head south on the A 816 to Lochgilphead. At Kilninver, turn right on the B 844 to Easdale. The road takes you across the famous Bridge Over The Atlantic. This graceful stone arch was built in 1791 and spans a very narrow arm of the sea separating the island of Seil from the mainland. On the far side of the bridge is a pub called Tigh an Truish, meaning 'House of the Trousers'. Legend has it that in the period following the 1745 uprising (see **Bonnie Prince Charlie**), when the wearing of the kilt was banned, islanders would stop at this hostelry to change into trousers before visiting the mainland. The road ends at the old slate-quarrying community of Easdale, where a passenger ferry (operates on demand 0730-2100 Mon.-Sat., 1030-1700 Sun., April-Sep., restricted service Oct.-Mar.) will take you to Easdale Island and its Folk Museum (1030-1730 Mon.-Sat., 1030-1630 Sun., April-Oct.; 75p, child 25p). Return to the main road and continue south, round the heads of lochs Melfort and Craignish, perhaps stopping to visit 16thC Carnasserie Castle (all times; free) or the carved 16thC gravestones and prehistoric standing stones and burial mounds around Kilmartin (all signposted), before reaching the wide, flat plain of Moine Mhor (Great Moss) on the right. This expanse of flat moor is broken by the little hill of Dunadd (turn right on minor road, signposted), which was the site of the capital of the kingdom of Dalriada, c.AD 500-800, from which arose the greater kingdom of Scotland. If you climb the hill you will see the few remains of the ancient fort, and carved into the bare rock of the summit, a boar, a footprint and a basin. It was here that the first kings of Scotland were crowned, sitting on the famous Stone of Destiny that was later moved across the country to Scone Palace (see **Perth**), before being stolen by Edward I and taken to Westminster, where it remains to this day. At Cairnbaan, the road joins the Crinan Canal, built 1793-1801, stretching 9 miles from Ardrishaig on Loch Fyne to Crinan on the Sound of Jura, saving fishing boats and yachts a long and hazardous trip around the Mull of Kintyre.

DETOURS: Turn right along the B 841 beside the canal, to a choice of three destinations: straight on to the Crinan Hotel at the end of the canal, where you can enjoy a delicious seafood dinner; turn right at Bellanoch, then left at the crossroads, and left again to reach Crinan

Ferry, opposite the hotel, where a string of sandy coves provides good picnic spots; or left on the B 8025 just beyond Bellanoch, to the pretty village of Tayvallich and the ruined 13thC chapel at Keillmore.

From Cairnbaan, it is only a few miles to Lochgilphead, which is where **EXCURSIONS 4A** and **4B** converge.

Lochgilphead. Pop: 2500. Full services. Tourist Information (April-Oct.), Lochnell St, tel: 0546-2344. Distances given below are from Lochgilphead. The A 83 leads south along the shore of Loch Fyne, passing the south end of the Crinan Canal at Ardrishaig, to the attractive fishing village of Tarbert.

DETOUR: A more interesting route is to turn right a few miles beyond the canal on the B 8024. This leads to Loch Caolisport, where a minor road on the right (signposted Ellary) leads in 3 miles to St. Columba's Cave. The cave lies behind a ruined 13thC chapel, and contains a rock shelf with altar and basin, above which are carved crosses. The cave was occupied from c.8000 BC, but is traditionally associated with the arrival of St. Columba (see A-Z) in Scotland in the 6thC. Return to the B 8024 and follow it around the Knapdale peninsula, enjoying the views across the sea to the mountains of Jura (see **Islay & Jura**), to rejoin the A 83, where you turn right.

Firth of Clyde

14 miles – Tarbert. Pop: 1500. Tourist Information (April-Oct.), Harbour St, tel: 08802-429. This attractive fishing village is now a popular centre for yachting and tourism, with a number of craft shops and seafood restaurants, the best of which are the Anchorage Restaurant and the Anchor Hotel. The village is particularly lively during the Clyde Cruising Club Yacht Races on the last weekend in May, and the Tarbert Fair at the end of July. Take the A 83 towards Campbeltown. A few miles out of Tarbert is the Kennacraig Ferry Terminal, where car ferries depart regularly for the islands of Islay and Jura, and at Tayinloan a small ferry will take you on the 20 min crossing to the lovely island of Gigha (4-6 crossings daily, first dep. from Tayinloan 0940, 0810 during school term, last dep. from Gigha 1600; £2.40 return). Here you can visit Achamore House Gardens (1000-dusk; £2, child £1), with their beautiful displays of rhododendrons, camellias and azaleas, the ruined 13thC church at Kilchattan, or enjoy a drink or a meal at the Gigha Hotel or Boathouse Bar. About 7 miles beyond Tayinloan a minor road on the left leads to Glenbarr and 18thC Glenbarr Abbey (1000-1700 Wed.-Mon., April-Oct.; £2, child £1), which is being restored and converted into a Clan Centre by the 5th Laird of Glenbarr. He provides an entertaining tour of his family seat, after which you can relax in the tearoom or wander in the grounds.

52 miles – Campbeltown. Pop: 6600. Tourist Information (all year), The Pier, tel: 0586-52056. A pleasant market town set around the head of Campbeltown Loch. Opposite the Tourist Information office is Campbeltown Cross, a richly carved 15thC stone cross, and nearby on the waterfront is Campbeltown Museum (1000-1300, 1400-1700 Mon.-Sat., plus 1800-2000 Mon. & Tue.; free), with exhibits on the history, culture, archaeology and geology of the Kintyre peninsula.

WALK: 2 hr. Drive along the road that follows the south shore of Campbeltown Loch to a parking place at the start of the gravel spit that leads out to Island Davaar. The spit is dry except at high tide (check time of low water with the Tourist Information office before making the walk). Cross the field to the shore and walk along the spit to the island, then follow the shore of the island along to the right, under the rocky cliffs. After a few hundred yards you will see some signs painted on the rock, guiding you to the Cave Painting. Here, set back on the left wall of a long, narrow cave, is a painting of the Crucifixion, completed in 1887 by Alexander MacKinnon. It has since been retouched, once by the artist himself in 1934, and more recently by a local artist, and is movingly rendered in blues, whites and mauves.

From Campbeltown drive 10 miles south to Southend, where there are some sandy beaches, and on across wild, moorland hills to the Mull of Kintyre itself, from where you can look across the North Channel to the coast of Northern Ireland, here only 12 miles away. Heading north from Campbeltown, take the B 842 up the east coast of the peninsula, with views across Kilbrannan Sound to the mountains of Arran (see **A-Z**). The road passes the ruins of Saddell Abbey (all times; free), founded in the 12thC and said to hold the (unmarked) grave of Somerled, first Lord of the Isles, before reaching attractive Carradale Bay, where there is a good beach. At Claonaig a car ferry crosses to Arran.

DETOUR: Drive northeast a few miles to Skipness, where you can explore the large 13thC Skipness Castle (presently undergoing restoration) and the nearby church of St. Brendan.

From Claonaig retrace your route north through Tarbert, or take the car ferry to Arran, and from there on to Ardrossan. From Ardrossan it is only 24 miles to Ayr (see **A-Z**), from where **EXCURSION 1** can be followed in reverse to the English border.

Stornoway

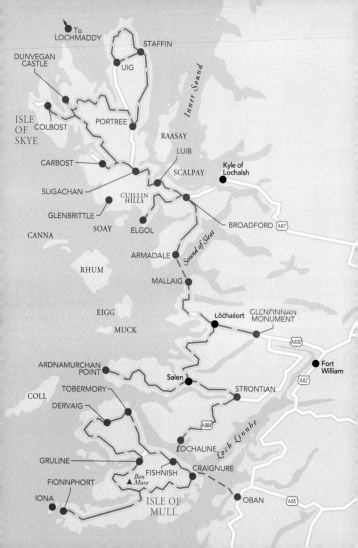

The Western Isles

Oban–Stornoway. Duration: 5-10 days.

As this route involves extensive use of car ferries, its timing should be planned in advance, especially if time is short. See **Ferries**.
Begin at Oban (see **A-Z**), reached via **EXCURSIONS 2** and **4B**, a 2-3 hr drive from Glasgow, and take the car ferry to Craignure on Mull. Mull is a scenic island of mountains, cliffs and moors, surrounded by rocky coves, beaches of white shell sand, and columnar, basalt crags.
The journey across the Firth of Lorn takes 40 min, and offers good views of Duart Castle on the final approach to Craignure. From just south of Craignure Pier, the Mull-West Highland Narrow Gauge Railway runs to Torosay Castle and Gardens (castle 1030-1700 April-Oct.; £2.50, child £1; gardens sunrise-sunset; £1, child 50p). The scenic journey takes 20 min (return £1.50, child £1, family £4), arriving at the Victorian castle, set in 12 acres of beautiful gardens. From Craignure, take the A 849 towards Fionnphort. After 2 miles or so, a minor road on the left leads out to Duart Castle (1030-1800 May-Sep.; £1.50, child 70p), seat of the Clan Maclean, spectacularly situated on a crag overlooking the sea. The ruined 13thC castle was restored in 1912 and is now home to the present chief of the clan. Follow the A 849 for 35 miles to Fionnphort, passing first through Glen More in the mountainous heart of the island, then along the north shore of the Ross of Mull peninsula.
WALK: 5 hr. A few miles after reaching the shores of Loch Scridain, just beyond the Pennyghael Hotel, a minor road on the left leads across the moors and down through lovely woods and past waterfalls to Carsaig Bay (where the road forks, take the left, uphill branch). Leave the car at the end of the road, and follow the path along the shore to the right, passing under huge cliffs (the going is sometimes rough, so wear good walking boots). After about 2 hr you will reach the spectacular Carsaig Arches, where the sea has carved the 755 ft-high basalt cliffs into awe-inspiring caves, buttresses and arches. Return by the same route.
The shores of the Ross of Mull contain many beautiful and secluded rocky coves, many with beaches of white shell sand, that can only be reached by foot. Turn off on any of the minor roads along the ross and explore. The main road ends at the village of Fionnphort (pronounced

'Finna-fort'), where a ferry will take you across the water to the famous island of Iona. The crossing takes 5 min and ferries depart at frequent intervals 0800-1900 Mon.-Sat. and hourly 1000-1700 Sun.; £1.30 return.

38 miles – Iona. This beautiful and historic island, only 3 miles by 1.5, is where St. Columba (see **A-Z**) came in AD 563 to establish a monastery, and to begin the spread of Christianity throughout Scotland. The main sights can be seen in 2-3 hr, but the rest of the island is a delight for walkers, bird-watchers, botanists and geologists. Walk up the main street opposite the jetty and turn right through the gate into the lovely grounds of the 13thC Benedictine nunnery, now mostly in ruins. At the far side is the little 14thC St. Ronan's Church, which has been restored to house a collection of sculpted medieval tombstones. Leave by the gate beside this church and go along the road, passing the 15thC Maclean's Cross on the left, then along to the right past the St. Columba Hotel to reach Iona Abbey (admission by donation). The mainly 16thC abbey buildings were restored in 1902-10, the surrounding monastic buildings in 1963-65, and are now home to the Iona Community, a religious group founded in 1938. To the right of the entrance gate is the Reilig Oran, the country's oldest Christian cemetery. The remains of 48 Scottish kings (including Duncan, killed by Macbeth – see **A-Z**), four Irish kings and eight Norwegian kings are said to lie here, though unfortunately their graves are no longer marked. The little Chapel of St. Oran (one of Columba's disciples) dates from the 11thC. In front of the main entrance to the abbey itself stand two magnificent 10thC Celtic crosses: St. John's to the left and St. Martin's to the right. Enter the main door of the abbey and pick up one of the self-guided tour leaflets (45p) before exploring the interior. In the cloisters to the left of the nave are the Community shop (1000-1700)

Mull from Iona

Duart Castle

and coffee house (1000-1700 Mon.-Sat., Mar.-Oct.). Services are held in the abbey at 1400 Mon.-Sat. in summer, with Holy Communion at 1030 Sun.

From Fionnphort, return along the A 849, but at the head of Loch Scridain turn left on the B 8035. This leads across the wild, cliff-bound Ardmeanach peninsula, then drops down to Loch na Keal, with views westward to the islands of Ulva and Staffa (see **A-Z**), where Fingal's Cave is to be found, before squeezing in between the sea and the steep basalt cliffs to reach Gruline. Here, a minor road on the right leads to the mausoleum of Lachlan Macquarie, the 'Father of Australia', who was born in 1761 on the nearby island of Ulva, and died here after retiring as Governor of New South Wales. Turn left on the B 8073, which follows the rugged west coast of northern Mull to windswept Calgary Bay (after which the Canadian city of Calgary is named), and on to the pretty village of Dervaig. On the right, immediately after the bridge, is a minor road leading to the Druimard Country House and Theatre Restaurant, next to which is the Mull Little Theatre, the smallest professional theatre in the country, with only 38 seats in the auditorium. There is a full summer programme of entertainment: for details call the box office, tel: 06884-245/234 (£4.50, child £3.50). Continue along the same road.

106 miles – Tobermory. Pop: 800. Tourist Information (April-Oct.), 48 Main St, tel: 06882-182. This pleasant, former fishing port was founded in 1788, and is now the main village on Mull, a centre for tourism, yachting and boat trips. Brightly painted houses ring the picturesque harbour, where in 1588 a Spanish galleon, fleeing the aftermath of the Armada, sought shelter and provisions. The ship sank and over the centuries many attempts have been made to recover the treasure she is said to have been carrying. So far only a few cannon and some coins have been found. The story of the galleon, and many other aspects of Mull's culture and history, are on display in the Mull Museum (1030-1630 Mon.-Fri., 1030-1330 Sat.; 50p, child 10p) on Main St opposite the pier. Three-hour cruises along the Sound of Mull on the *Girl Deborah* depart daily from Macbrayne's Pier at the north end of Main St (1030 & 1430 Mar.-Sep.; £10, child £6). An infrequent car ferry service (Mon., Wed. & Sat.) connects Tobermory with Oban, Coll and Tiree (see **A-Z**), and a regular passenger ferry links the town with Kilchoan (see page 84) on the Ardnamurchan peninsula (Mon.-Sat.); for details, tel: 0688-2017. From Tobermory follow the A 848 along the Sound of Mull through attractive Salen Bay.

122 miles – Fishnish. Here a car ferry operates between Mull and Lochaline on the mainland. The crossing takes 15 min and there are frequent sailings 0700-1900 Mon.-Sat., and hourly sailings 1020-1620 Sun. (one-way, car £5.65, passenger £1.25). For details, tel: 0631-62285. Before leaving Lochaline, drive up to Keil Church above the village. The churchyard contains a 15thC Celtic cross and commands a splendid view over the Sound of Mull, with 14thC Ardtornish Castle prominent a few miles to the southeast. Take the A 884 from Lochaline along lovely, wooded Gleann Geal and over the hills to the head of Loch Sunart, where you turn left on the A 861 through Strontian (Tourist Information, June-Sep., tel: 0967-2131) and on to Salen.

DETOUR: From Salen the B 8007, one of Scotland's most scenic roads, snakes 23 miles through rhododendron-clad hillsides and beautiful hill scenery to the gale-worn lighthouse on Ardnamurchan Point, the most westerly point on the British mainland (it projects a full 23 miles further west than Land's End). There is a hotel and limited camping at Kilchoan (connected to Tobermory on Mull by a regular passenger ferry, see page 83), and nearby are the ruins of 13thC Mingary Castle (all times; free). About a mile beyond Kilchoan, on the way out to the lighthouse, a minor road on the right leads to the gorgeous, white-sand beach of Sanna Bay.

The A 861 continues north from Salen. A mile or so beyond Acharacle, just after the bridge over the River Shiel, take a minor road on the left (signposted Dorlin), that winds along a rocky ledge beside the river, overhung by trees, moss and ferns, before coming out after 2 miles at a parking place by the shores of Loch Moidart. The ruined 14thC Castle Tioram, ancient seat of the Macdonalds of Clanranald, sits romantically on a small islet near the shore, and is accessible via a sand spit except at high water. The main road leads on around the north shore of Loch Moidart – where five prominent beech trees are survivors of the original seven planted to commemorate the Seven Men of Moidart who accompanied Bonnie Prince Charlie (see **A-Z**) on his voyage from France – and on to Lochailort where it meets the A 830.

DETOUR: Turn right towards Fort William (see **EXCURSION 2**, **A-Z**), passing the famous Glenfinnan Monument at the north end of Loch Shiel, which commemorates the raising of Prince Charlie's standard near here in 1745. Note that the statue on top of the monument is not of the prince; it is representative of the brave Highlanders who fought for his cause. The adjacent Visitor Centre (1000-1730 April, May & Oct., 0930-1830 June-Sep.; 90p, child 50p) tells the story of the Prince's subsequent campaign to regain the Scottish throne, ending with inglorious defeat at Culloden (see **EXCURSION 8**).

To continue to the Western Isles, turn left at Lochailort towards Mallaig. On the way is Loch Morar, Britain's deepest at 1017 ft, and reputedly the home of another monster, Morag.

192 miles – Mallaig. Pop: 1000. Tourist Information (April-Sep.), Railway Station, tel: 0687-2170. Mallaig lies at the end of the road and railway from Fort William and Glasgow, and is an important fishing port and ferry terminal. Passenger ferries serve the Small Isles (see **A-Z**), and a car ferry makes the 30 min crossing to Armadale on Skye. For details, tel: 0687-2403.

Cross over the sea to Skye, christened 'Skuye' (Island of Clouds) by the invading Norsemen, a name whose aptness will soon become apparent to the visitor. Skye is the largest and most popular of Scotland's islands, mostly given over to crofting. Gaelic is widely spoken, and both here and in the Outer Hebrides (see **Hebrides**) you will find that roadsigns and other notices are bilingual.

Just outside Armadale is the Clan Donald Centre, where the restored Armadale Castle houses the Museum of the Isles (0930-1730 April-Oct.; £2, child £1.50), telling the story of Clan Donald and the Lords of the Isles: there are also a pleasant restaurant, tearoom and shop. Follow the A 851 along the Sleat peninsula to the A 850 (turn right here for the ferry to Kyle of Lochalsh and the start of **EXCURSION 6**) and the long, straggling, village of Broadford (Tourist Information, April-Sep., tel: 04712-361).

DETOUR: Turn left on the A 881, which leads for 14 miles through beautiful scenery to the village of Elgol, from where you can enjoy views to the peaks of the Cuillin and the island of Rhum.

WALK: 6 hr. A coastal footpath leads north from Elgol for 3 miles to Camasunary, and from there continues another 3 miles, past a difficult section of rock-scrambling called the Bad Step, to remote Loch Coruisk in the heart of the Cuillin. This walk leads through wild and magnificent scenery, but should only be attempted by experienced walkers. Coruisk can be more easily reached from Elgol by boat.

North of Broadford, the main road sticks to the east coast of Skye and turns sharply left at the mouth of Loch Ainort, with good views to the conical peaks of the Cuillins. At Luib there is a Folk Museum (1000-1800; 70p, child free), housed in an old thatched crofter's house and furnished with 19thC objects and agricultural implements. The road passes the ferry to the nearby island of Raasay at Sconser, before reaching the junction at Sligachan. The hotel and camp site here form a centre for climbing in the Cuillin mountains, whose jagged, rocky peaks rise impressively to the south. Turn left on the A 863, which leads along the west coast of the island, with good views of sea-lochs and the flat-topped hills called Macleod's Tables.

DETOUR: Six miles from Sligachan the B 8009 on the left leads to Carbost, where there is the Talisker Distillery (1000-1200, 1400-1600 Mon.-Fri.). Before Carbost, a minor road forks left to Glenbrittle, another centre for exploring the Cuillin, where there are a large camp site and a youth hostel.

Dunvegan Castle

247 miles – Dunvegan Castle (1000-1730 Mon.-Sat., Mar.-Oct.; £3.30, child £1.70). A well-known tourist attraction which has been the seat of the chiefs of Clan Macleod for over 700 years. There is much of interest on display, including the Fairy Flag, a silken banner over 1200 years old that is reputed to have the magical power to save the clan from peril three times – it has been used twice already – and weapons, furniture, paintings, books and documents tracing the history of the clan over 30 generations. Just before Dunvegan village, the B 884 on the left leads 10 miles to the wild cliff scenery of Neist Point, passing on the way Colbost Folk Museum (1000-1800; 70p, child free) and the road to Husabost, on which is the MacCrimmon Piping Centre (1000-1800 Mon.-Sat., 1400-1800 Sun.; 75p, child 10p), a museum devoted to the famous family of pipers who played for the chiefs of Clan Macleod. From Dunvegan take the A 850.

270 miles – Portree. Pop: 1500. Tourist Information (all year), Meall House, tel: 0478-2137. Portree is the principal village on Skye, with hotels, restaurants, shops, banks, etc. The Portree House Hotel, up the hill behind the town, offers good bar lunches and dinners, or try the Ben Tianavaig Bistro above the harbour, which serves excellent seafood and vegetarian dishes. Take the A 855 towards Staffin. Soon the serrated outline of The Storr appears on the left.

WALK: 2 hr. This jumble of crags and pinnacles includes the prominent, 165 ft-high finger of the Old Man of Storr, first climbed in 1955. It can be reached by a path along the north side of the forestry plantation at the end of Loch Leathan.

The road follows the east coast of the Trotternish peninsula through fertile farmland backed by cliffs of volcanic rock: spectacular sea cliffs and waterfalls can be seen at the Kilt Rock viewpoint. A few miles beyond Staffin a minor road on the right cuts across the peninsula to Uig, passing on the way a parking place from which a footpath leads uphill to the weird pinnacles of The Quiraing, where you can admire

Standing Stones, Callanish

the 100 ft-tall Needle, an unnaturally flat meadow called The Table and good views across the sea to Torridon. The main road continues around the northern tip of the peninsula to the Kilmuir Croft Museum (0900-1730 Mon.-Sat., April-Oct.; £1, child 50p) and the grave of Flora Macdonald (see **Bonnie Prince Charlie**), then sweeps down to the bay of Uig.

302 miles – Uig. A car ferry runs from Uig to Tarbert on Harris, and Lochmaddy on North Uist, in the Outer Hebrides (one-way, car £21.80-32.30, passenger £5.40). For details, tel: 047042-219.

The Outer Hebrides form a 130 mile-long island chain off the north-west coast of Scotland. Of over 200 islands only 13 are inhabited, and 80% of the 31,000 population lives on the largest island, Lewis and Harris. The scenery is often wild and bleak, occasionally relieved by splashes of green around the crofting communities, and by the splendid golden-sand beaches of the west coasts. The islanders make a living from crofting, fishing and cottage industries like the weaving of Harris Tweed, and are predominantly Gaelic-speaking. Lewis, Harris and North Uist form a stronghold of the Free Presbyterian Church, which strictly observes the Sabbath: on Sun. all shops, bars, restaurants and public services close down and this should be allowed for in planning a trip. South Uist and Barra are predominantly Roman Catholic and Sun. is somewhat livelier on these islands (see **Hebrides**).

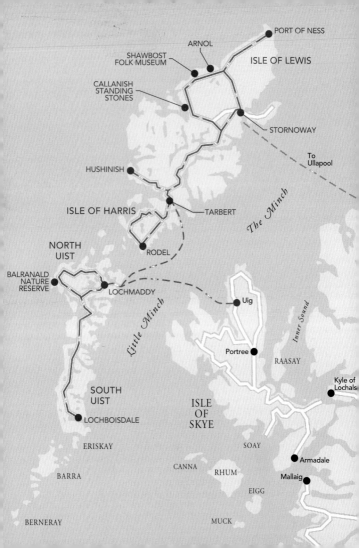

Take the ferry to Lochmaddy (Tourist Information, April-Sep., above the pier, tel: 08763-321). Follow the A 865, which loops around the coast of North Uist before heading south through Benbecula and South Uist (the islands are connected by causeways) to reach Lochboisdale, 46 miles away. At Kilphedder there is a stone cross on a rise to the right of the road, a memorial to a local doctor, from where you can enjoy a view northwest to the serrated Haskeir Islands and beyond to the hazy outlines of St. Kilda, 41 miles away. A few miles further on, turn right at Tigharry to visit Balranald Nature Reserve, owned by the RSPB (Ionad Fiosrachaidh Visitor Centre, 1000-1300 Sat.-Wed.; free). The road skirts the sandy coastline, passing many ruined blackhouses (old, turf-roofed crofter's cottages), before turning south and crossing tidal flats to Benbecula.

Loop right from the main road on the B 892 which passes through Balivanich, the island's main village, home to many of the servicemen who work at the RAF airfield and the missile range on South Uist. At Liniclate, just before you rejoin the main road, is the Dark Island Hotel, reckoned to be the best in the Hebrides, where you can indulge yourself in delicious, if expensive, local venison, scallops and lobster.

The road now crosses another causeway to South Uist, and yet another over freshwater Loch Bee, with views ahead to the hills of Hecla and Ben Mhor, rising to over 1900 ft. On the hillside beyond Loch Bee stands the 33 ft-tall statue of the Madonna and Child, Our Lady of the Isles, erected by the Catholic community in 1957. A ruined cottage to the right of the road just before Mingary has a cairn commemorating it as the birthplace of Flora Macdonald.

348 miles – Lochboisdale. Tourist Information (April-Sep.), Ferry Pier, tel: 08784-286. The chief village on South Uist. From here you can catch a car ferry to Castlebay on Barra, or to Oban, or drive to Ludag on the south coast and catch a passenger ferry to Eoligarry at the northern tip of Barra, from where it is a short walk to Cille Bharra, with its three 12thC chapels. The author Compton Mackenzie is buried here; the island of Eriskay, off Ludag, was the setting for his famous book *Whisky Galore*. The Prince's Strand, on the west side of Eriskay, is where Prince Charlie first set foot on Scottish soil. To continue this excursion, return to Lochmaddy and take the ferry to Tarbert on Harris.

384 miles – Tarbert (Tairbeart). Tourist Information (April-Oct.), behind the pier, tel: 0859-2011. The chief village of Harris. There are a couple of shops, a post office, banks and a petrol station. The delightful Rose Villa Tearoom (on the right-hand side of the road as you leave the pier) is a welcome haven on a rainy day.

DETOUR: South Harris, 40 miles. From Tarbert, go left on the A 859 for 4 miles, then left on a minor road (the Golden Road, so named because of the high cost of its construction). This road twists and turns for 12 miles down the wild east coast of Harris, through a landscape of rough, hillocky gneiss, sprinkled with lochans and deeply indented by the sea. The bleakness is brightened here and there by a splash of green around the crofting communities. At Rodel (Roghadal) is the neat little 15th-16thC church of St. Clement. Return by the west coast road (much faster than the east) to Tarbert, passing beautiful sandy beaches at Scarastavore, Borve (Buirgh) and Seilebost, separated by stretches of low, shelving rocky coast.

The A 859 leads north from Tarbert to Stornoway, through wild hills and across desolate moors.

DETOUR: Three miles out of Tarbert the B 887 on the left leads along the north shore of West Loch Tarbert. This passes an old whaling station at Bunavoneader, built by the Norwegians in 1912 but abandoned in the 1930s. There are dramatic views into the mountainous Forest of Harris to the north, before you arrive at the attractive Amhuinnsuidhe Castle. The road passes through a white iron gate, along the bank of a salmon stream tumbling to the sea, and goes right past the front door of the castle, which is used as a hunting and fishing lodge (closed to the public), before leaving through an ornamental, turreted arch. The road continues as far as Hushinish (Huisnis), where there is an attractive sandy beach. Return to the A 859 by the same route.

421 miles – Stornoway (Steornabhagh). Pop: 8000. Tourist Information (all year), 4 South Beach St, tel: 0851-3088. The main town of the Outer Hebrides is an unexpected oasis of trees, parkland and cosy streets amid the surrounding bleakness of moor and mountain. From the Tourist Information office turn left along the waterfront to the Town Hall on the left at Cromwell St. This houses the Museum Nan Eilean (1000-1230, 1400-1730 Tue.-Sat., June-Aug., 1400-1700 Tue.-

Sat., Sep.-May; free), which illustrates the history of Lewis and the daily life of its inhabitants, and An Lanntair Art Gallery (1000-1800 Mon.-Sat.; free). Across the river from the town is Lews Castle, now a college, surrounded by attractive parkland; a good place for a walk or a picnic. About 4 miles east of town (take the A 866 to Eye peninsula, but turn left after the narrow neck of land) is the 14thC St. Columba's Church, in a graveyard. Inside are a stone effigy of Roderic MacLeod and a beautifully carved stone slab, possibly from his daughter's grave. From the roundabout north of town, take the A 857 to Barvas (Barabhas), across the huge desolate peat moor that occupies most of the northern part of Lewis.

DETOUR: From Barvas, it is 12 miles to Port of Ness (Port Nis) and the Butt of Lewis, the most northerly point on the island. On the way is the prehistoric burial cairn of Steinacleit Stone Circle at Shader.

Turn left on the A 858 to Shawbost. At Arnol is a restored blackhouse (HS site, see **Opening Times**, but closed 1300-1400 & Sun.; 60p, child 30p) which contains much of its original furniture. The Folk Museum (0900-1800 Mon.-Sat., April-Nov.; donation) at Shawbost is housed in an old church just before the cattle grid in the middle of the village. It was put together by local school children and depicts the traditional life style of the people of Lewis. A minor road on the right leads to Dalmore, where there is a good, sandy beach, and a few miles further on another minor road leads to Dun Carloway, the best-preserved broch (see **A-Z**) in the Hebrides. The Standing Stones at Callanish are perhaps the best-known prehistoric site in the Hebrides: the atmospheric setting is well worth a visit. There are 48 stones, all of beautifully banded Lewisean gneiss, set in the form of a cross and circle on a hillock above the loch. Continue to Stornoway, where the excursion ends (496 miles).

From Stornoway you can either return to Tarbert and take the ferry back to Uig on Skye, or take the car ferry from Stornoway to the mainland at Ullapool in order to join **EXCURSION 6**. The latter ferry runs daily Mon.-Sat. (one-way, car £30.50-44.60, passenger £7.60). For details, tel: 0851-2361.

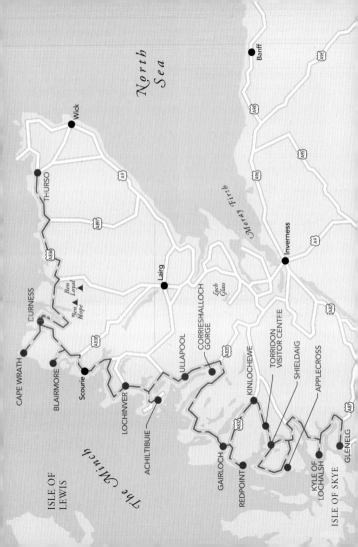

Kyle of Lochalsh–Thurso/Orkney. Duration: 2-5 days.

Begin at Kyle of Lochalsh, reached by ferry from Skye (see **EXCURSION 5**) or from Invergarry (see **EXCURSION 2**) via the A 87. The latter route descends through lovely Glen Shiel in Kintail and passes the famous Eilan Donan Castle (1000-1800 Easter-Sep.; £1), immortalized in calendars and on the lids of souvenir shortbread tins.

DETOUR: From Shiel Bridge take the minor road to Glenelg. This climbs steeply to the Pass of Mam Ratachan, 1116 ft above sea level, offering splendid views of the peaks known as The Five Sisters of Kintail, before descending into the lovely wooded valley of Glen More to reach the village of Glenelg after 12 miles. At nearby Kylerhea a car ferry (July & Aug.) makes the 5 min crossing to Skye. Fork left at Glenelg and turn left again to visit the interesting brochs (see **A-Z**) of Dun Telve and Dun Troddan (all times; free). There are many pleasant walks in the surrounding area.

Kyle of Lochalsh. Pop: 700. Tourist Information (April-Oct.), Car Park, tel: 0599-4276. Terminus of the West Highland railway line and site of the short car ferry crossing to Skye (frequent daily service, crossing time 5 min; one-way, car £4.50, passenger free). Take the minor road opposite the ferry slip that leads north through unexpectedly green and fertile scenery to the picture-postcard village of Plockton, set around an attractive bay. You can hire a sailing dinghy here or take a boat trip to see seals and other wildlife. Follow the road to Achmore and join the A 890, which leads around the head of Loch Carron, where you should turn left on the A 899. From Kishorn the main road leads 10 miles to Shieldaig, but a far more interesting route is the 35 miles of minor road via Applecross. This spectacular road (not suitable

Plockton

for caravans) climbs over the 2053 ft-high Bealach na Bà (Pass of the Cattle), before descending more gently to the coast at the village of Applecross. Turn right here on the coast road, with views across to Raasay and Skye, passing many ruined crofts. At Fearnmore the mountains of Torridon come into view as the road swings east, rejoining the main road at Shieldaig.

70 miles – Torridon Visitor Centre (1000-1800 Mon.-Sat., 1400-1800 Sun., June-Sep.; 60p, child 30p). A deer museum with displays illustrating local wildlife. The surrounding area contains some of the most impressive mountain scenery in Britain and provides excellent hill walking for the experienced walker. The principal peaks are Liathach (3456 ft), whose great bulk looms above the visitor centre, and Beinn Eighe (3309 ft) at the head of the glen. The latter forms part of Beinn Eighe National Nature Reserve, Britain's first, with much of interest for walkers, bird-watchers and geologists. The reserve has its own visitor centre at Aultroy near Kinlochewe. Nearby is a circular, self-guided Mountain Walk, with signs pointing out items of natural and geological interest (3 hr). At Kinlochewe turn left on the A 832 along the shore of lovely Loch Maree, with the distinctive outline of Slioch (3217 ft) across the water. Near Slattadale, a car park on the left is the starting point for a forest walk to Victoria Falls, named after Queen Victoria, who visited the area in 1877.

DETOUR: Turn left on the B 8056 which leads in 9 miles to the beautiful sandy beach of Redpoint, a perfect picnic spot, with views to the hills of northern Skye and the Outer Hebrides (see **Hebrides**).

101 miles – Gairloch. Pop: 150. Tourist Information (all year), tel: 0445-2130. A popular holiday centre strung out around the wide bay. The Gairloch Heritage Museum (1000-1700 Easter-Sep.; 50p, child 10p) has a series of interesting exhibits illustrating different aspects of West Highland life over the past few hundred years. The road between Gairloch and Poolewe offers splendid views eastward into the mountains north of Loch Maree: near Loch Tollaidh is the beginning of a pleasant 5 mile footpath along the banks of Loch Maree to Slattadale. Just beyond Poolewe are the famous Inverewe Gardens (0930-sunset; £2.20, child £1.10), where palm trees and other exotic plants flourish in the mild climate. The road now touches Gruinard Bay, which is

ringed by sandy beaches (Gruinard Island, in the middle of the bay, has recently been declared safe again, after being contaminated with anthrax during World War II tests of chemical weapons), before climbing above Little Loch Broom and dropping down to the Corrieshalloch Gorge. Turn left on the A 835 and stop at the car park to take a stroll down to the viewing platforms and suspension bridge, where you can get a close look at the spectacular, 200 ft-deep gorge and the 150 ft Falls of Measach.

155 miles – Ullapool. Pop: 800. Tourist Information (April-Oct.), West Shore St, tel: 0854-2135. A fishing port, tourist centre and the terminal for the car ferry to Stornoway (see **EXCURSION 5**). Boat trips to the beautiful Summer Isles are available from the pier, and at nearby Ardmair you can hire canoes, sailboards, rowing boats, motor boats and fishing

tackle. For details, tel: 0854-2054. About 9 miles north of Ullapool, turn left on the minor road to Achiltibuie. This leads into Inverpolly Nature Reserve and some magnificent mountain scenery. The road passes directly beneath the jagged sandstone crest of Stac Pollaidh, a steep climb from the parking place by Loch Lurgainn (3 hr round trip; experienced hill walkers only). Detour to the village of Achiltibuie for boat trips to the Summer Isles or to visit the Hydroponicum (guided tours 1000, 1200, 1400 & 1700 April-Oct.; £4, child £2.50), a unique, high-tech greenhouse where plants are grown using aquaculture – no soil is required. All kinds of fruit are grown, from bananas to lemons and grapefruit. Continue on the minor road (unsuitable for caravans) that twists through the hills to Lochinver.

185 miles – Lochinver. Pop: 300. Tourist Information (April-Oct.), Main St, tel: 05714-330. A pleasant lochside village with a small supermarket, shops and a restaurant, and famous for splendid views of the strange-shaped mountains of Assynt that rise inland, especially the great sugar loaf of Suilven. Take the B 869 which follows the coast round to Eddrachillis Bay, passing a number of good, sandy beaches at Achmelvich, Clachtoll and Clashnessie, before rejoining the main road a few miles before the modern Kylesku Bridge, under the gullied flanks of Quinag (2653 ft). From the old ferry pier near the bridge, wildlife cruises depart to explore Loch Glencoul (1100, 1400 & 1600 Mon.-Fri., 1400 & 1600 Sat. & Sun.; £5, child £2.50). Beyond Scourie, a minor road on the left leads to Tarbet, from where a ferry will take you to Handa Island Nature Reserve (daily from 1000, tel: 0971-2156). The island's cliffs teem with seabirds during the nesting season.

WALK: 3-4 hr. Take the B 801 from Rhiconich to Kinlochbervie (an important fishing port) and on to Blairmore, where a signpost on the

right indicates a farm track leading to Sandwood Bay. Leave your car here and follow the track for 2 miles, then its continuation as a footpath for another 2 miles to reach a beautiful, sandy beach. Tradition has it that this remote strand, guarded by the sea stack of Am Buachaillo (The Herdsman) at its southern end, is a favourite haunt of mermaids.

245 miles – Durness. Tourist Information (April-Oct.), tel: 097181-259. Scotland's most northwesterly village, with a youth hostel and camp site. Its main attraction is Smoo Cave, a huge limestone cavern cut into the sea cliffs below the road just east of the village. Nearby are the sand dunes of scenic Balnakeil Bay, with its ruined 17thC church, and Balnakeil Craft Village, where a community of artists and craftspeople have set up studios and workshops. You can watch them at work, and buy crafts and paintings straight from the artist. Just south of Durness is a passenger ferry which will take you across the Kyle of Durness, from where you can continue 8 miles by minibus to Cape Wrath, the wild, cliff-bound, northwestern extremity of the Scottish mainland. The road now follows the north coast round Loch Eriboll and across the causeway at the Kyle of Tongue, with the peaks of Ben Hope (3040 ft) and Ben Loyal off to the right. There are some beautiful beaches along this remote coast, notably at Bettyhill, Strathy and Melvich. The land gets flatter and more fertile as you enter Caithness, and the white dome of Dounreay Nuclear Power Station rises on the left. There is a Visitor Centre (0900-1630 Easter-Sep.; free) at Dounreay, which explains how nuclear power is generated, and guided tours of the reactor. A few more miles bring you to Thurso, where the excursion ends (326 miles). Ferries leave Scrabster, near Thurso, for Orkney, the next part of the excursion, or alternatively you can follow **EXCURSION 7** along the coast through Caithness to Inverness.

ORKNEY

ROUSAY

EDAY

BROUGH
OF BIRSAY

BROCH OF
GURNESS

MAINLAND

SKARA BRAE

SHAPINSAY

MAES
HOWE

STROMNESS

STONES OF
STENNESS

KIRKWALL

ORPHIR

HOUTON

*Scapa
Flow*

ITALIAN
CHAPEL

OLD
MAN
OF HOY

RACKWICK

HOY

BURRAY

FLOTTA

ST. MARGARET'S
HOPE

SOUTH
RONALDSAY

Burwick

STROMA

John o'Groats

A836

Thurso

Orkney

Duration: 1 day.

P&O Scottish Ferries operates car ferries from Aberdeen to Stromness and on to Lerwick (one dep., weekdays only, passage time 8 hr; return £87-105 car, £47-106 passenger), and from Scrabster (near Thurso) to Stromness (1-3 deps daily, no Sun. sailings Nov.-Mar., passage time 1 hr 50 min; return £45-61 car, £19 passenger). A passenger ferry runs between John o'Groats and Burwick, South Ronaldsay, with a bus connection to Kirkwall and Stromness (1-3 deps daily April-Sep., passage time 45 min; return £14, or £16 inc. bus to Kirkwall).

The islands of Orkney are situated off the northeast tip of Scotland, separated from the mainland by the 8 miles of the Pentland Firth. There are over 70 islands, most of them small and uninhabited, a paradise for many species of seabird. The principal island is Mainland, about 20 miles long, which has the two main towns of Kirkwall and Stromness. It is connected to the southern islands of Burray and South Ronaldsay by causeways, and by ferry services to the larger inhabited islands. The islands are worth a holiday in themselves, but for the traveller with limited time this tour takes in the principal sights on Mainland and can be completed in a day, starting and finishing at Stromness.

Stromness. Pop: 1800. Tourist Information (all year), quayside opposite the pier, tel: 0856-850716. Once a thriving whaling port and outpost of the Hudson Bay Co., the town is clustered along the long, narrow, winding Main St paved with local flagstone. Walking south from the Tourist Information office you will find on your left the Pier Arts Centre (1030-1230, 1330-1700 Tue.-Sat., 1400-1700 Sun., July & Aug.; free), a gallery housing a collection of 20thC British art, and other, changing exhibitions. Four hundred yards from the pier on the right is Leslie's

Skara Brae

Close, with the Hamnavoe Restaurant, an excellent spot for dinner, with a menu based on freshly prepared local produce. Stromness Museum (1100-1230, 1330-1700 Mon.-Wed., Fri. & Sat., 1100-1300 Thu.; 40p, child 20p) is about 800 yd south of the ferry pier. It was founded in 1837 and has occupied its present premises since 1858. There are interesting exhibits on the scuttling of the German High Fleet in Scapa Flow in 1919, and the intimate association between Orkney and the Hudson Bay Co., plus a small natural history collection. The town holds an annual gala known as Shopping Week, which begins in the 3rd week in July, with music, dancing, fêtes, events, etc. From Stromness leave by the A 965, go left on the A 967 to Birsay, and left again on the B 9056 to Skaill, following signs to Skara Brae.

7 miles – Skara Brae (HS site, see **Opening Times**, but closed 1230-1330; £1.20, child 60p). Set on the picturesque Bay of Skaill, this is the best-preserved prehistoric village in northern Europe, dating from around 3100-2500 BC. The site is especially interesting as it gives some insight into the daily lives of its Neolithic inhabitants. The cheery custodians will give an informative guided tour, free.

DETOUR: From here you can make a circuit of the north part of Mainland, taking in the interesting prehistoric sites at the Brough of Birsay and Broch of Gurness, the latter being the best-preserved broch (see **A-Z**) in Orkney.

From Skara Brae, head back southeast on the B 9056 to look at the atmospheric stone circles on the spit of land between the lochs of Stenness and Harray – the Ring of Brogar and the Stones of Stenness (all times; free) – before going on to the enormous burial mound of Maes Howe.

13 miles – Maes Howe (HS site, see **Opening Times**; £1, child 50p). Pay for your ticket at the kiosk beside the parking area and wait for the custodian to accompany you to the mound and show you round. The chambered tomb within is the best example of its kind in Europe. The large central chamber with its corbelled roof is approached along a low, narrow passage. Three burial vaults lead off the other walls of the chamber. Interest is added by the presence of runic inscriptions on the walls, made by Vikings who broke into the tomb in the 12thC. The great mound is an atmospheric spot at sunset, when you can look across the Loch of Harray to the nearby stone circles. Follow the A 965 to Kirkwall.

22 miles – Kirkwall. Pop: 6700. Tourist Information (all year), Broad St, tel: 0856-2856. Orkney's principal town is dominated by the impressive pink and yellow masonry of St. Magnus' Cathedral (0900-1300, 1400-1700 Mon.-Sat., May-Aug.; free), built in the 12th-15thC and housing the relics of SS Magnus and Rognvald. Next to the cathedral are the imposing ruins of the 12thC Bishop's Palace (with a good view from the top of the tower) and early-17thC Earl's Palace (HS site, see **Opening Times**; 60p, child 30p). Across the street from the cathedral is the excellent Tankerness House Museum (1030-1230, 1330-1700 Mon.-Sat., 1400-1700 Sun., May-Sep.; £1, child free), which covers many aspects of Orkney's history. On the road out of town towards St. Margaret's Hope (A 961) is the Highland Park Distillery, Holm Rd (1000-1600 Mon.-Fri., April-Sep., plus 1000-1200 Sat., June-Aug., by arrangement Oct.-Mar.; free). The guided tour is one of the best distillery tours in the country, with the opportunity to sample the whisky while enjoying a very professional audio-visual presentation on the history of the islands.

DETOUR: The road continues for 20 miles south to Burwick on South Ronaldsay where there is a passenger ferry to John o'Groats (see page 105). On the way you can visit the Italian Chapel (all times; free) on

Lamb Holm, a beautiful chapel built by Italian prisoners of war in 1943. It is housed in a tiny Nissen hut and was lovingly fashioned from scrap metal, concrete and any other odds and ends the prisoners could find. The road passes over causeways made from huge concrete blocks. These are known as the Churchill Barriers and were built during World War II to keep submarines out of Scapa Flow. The wrecks of old block ships (which were sunk on purpose to block the passages before the construction of the barriers) can be seen rusting in the shallows nearby. At St. Margaret's Hope on South Ronaldsay is the Orkney Wireless Museum (1000-1900 April-Sep.; 50p, child 25p), dedicated to wartime communications.

From Kirkwall return to Stromness by the A 964, which skirts the shore of Scapa Flow, Orkney's great natural harbour, which formed an important naval base during both World Wars. In 1919 the German High Fleet, captured by the British, was scuttled here in an act of defiance. Most of the ships were salvaged, but seven still lie on the sea bed, a continuing attraction for scuba divers from all over the world. At Orphir, about 9 miles from Kirkwall, is the ruin of the 12thC Orphir Church, unusual in being Scotland's only circular medieval church. At Houton is the car ferry to Hoy.

DETOUR: If you have time to spare, the island of Hoy is well worth a visit. In addition to the car ferry from Houton, there is a regular passenger ferry from Stromness. Hoy is the only really hilly island in Orkney, and offers excellent walking.

WALK: A recommended short walk follows a well-worn path from beautiful Rackwick Bay for 2 miles or so to the cliff top opposite the Old Man of Hoy, at 450 ft the highest sea stack in the British Isles. The trip round the island from Moaness Pier (where the Stromness ferry drops you off) is 8-10 miles.

Old Man of Hoy

Stromness Regatta

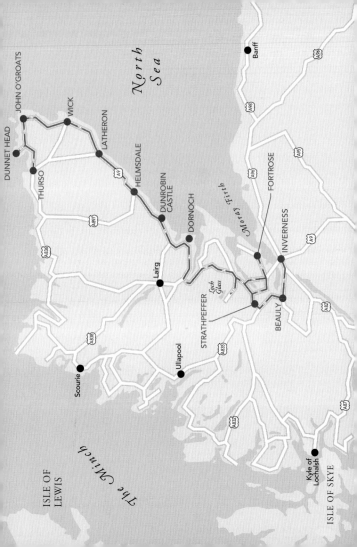

Caithness

Thurso–Inverness. Duration: 1-2 days.

Thurso. Pop: 9000. Tourist Information (April-Oct.), Riverside, tel: 0847-62371. The principal town of Scotland's north coast. Things to see include the ruins of the 12th-13thC St. Peter's Church, rebuilt in the 17thC, and Thurso Heritage Museum (1000-1300, 1400-1700 Mon.-Sat., June-Sep.; 50p, child 10p) in the Town Hall. Two miles beyond Thurso is Scrabster, the point of departure for the car ferry to Stromness in Orkney (see **EXCURSION 6**). Follow the A 836 east out of the town, past Castletown. The road flanks the sandy beach of Dunnet Bay. Ahead of you is the stark, humpbacked outline of Dunnet Head, dropping vertically into the sea. At this point you can go down the B 855 (turning left off the main road) until you come to a car park and viewpoint indicator near the lighthouse. This is the British mainland's most northerly point and there are grand views to Orkney, dominated by the hills of Hoy, and west along the coast to Ben Loyal and Ben Hope. Turn back to the A 836, travelling east.

18 miles – John o'Groats. Tourist Information (April-Oct.), tel: 095581-373. The Scottish equivalent of Land's End. There are hotels, B&Bs, a restaurant, pub, and souvenir and craft shops. In summer a passenger ferry runs to Burwick on South Ronaldsay (see **EXCURSION 6**). A minor road on the left leads to the white lighthouse at Duncansby Head, with views across the swirling tide races of the Pentland Firth, one of Britain's most treacherous stretches of water.

WALK: 45 min. From the car park at Duncansby Head, a signposted footpath runs south along the cliff tops for about three-quarters of a mile to the spectacular rock needles of the Stacks of Duncansby, passing seabird-haunted cliffs and impressive rock scenery.

Head south on the A 9. The road climbs onto a desolate moor, with a magnificent view back over the Pentland Firth and Stroma Island to the low outline of Orkney, then sweeps down to the coast, passing the ruins of a broch (see **A-Z**) near Nybster and the sandy links of Reiss.

35 miles – Wick (see **A-Z**). Continue south on the A 9 past the turn-offs to the right to the prehistoric sites of the Hill o'Many Stanes and the Grey Cairns of Camster.

52 miles – Latheron. The Clan Gunn Heritage Centre (1100-1700

Mon.-Sat., June-Sep.; £1, child 60p), housed in the 18thC Latheron Parish Church, records the history of the Clan Gunn, and includes genealogical and historical records relating to the clan. Three miles further on, the Lhaidhay Croft Museum (0900-1700 Easter-Sep.; 50p, child 20p) is a restored thatched croft containing a wide-ranging collection of everyday household objects and farm implements from the late 19th-early 20thC. There is an interesting original 'cruck' roof in the neighbouring byre, built entirely from driftwood because of a lack of timber in the area.

56 miles – Dunbeath Heritage Centre (1000-1700 Mon.-Sat., 1100-1800 Sun., May-Sep.; Mon.-Fri., April; closed 1300-1400 April & May; £1.50, child 50p). Reached by turning left at Dunbeath village, this is another collection of tableaux displaying local history and wildlife. On a clear day it is possible to see the Beatrice Oilfield offshore from the centre.

72 miles – Helmsdale. Pop: 1000. Tourist Information (April-Sep.), Couper Park, tel: 04312-640. Cross the bridge on the main road and turn right into this small fishing village to find the Timespan Visitor Centre (1000-1700 Mon.-Sat., 1400-1700 Sun., mid May-mid Oct.; £1.75, child 75p), where local history, including the Kildonan Gold Rush, is displayed through a series of tableaux and audio-visual presentations. The road running south from here to the fishing village of Brora climbs above the cliff-lined coast, occasionally sweeping down to small towns and villages at the mouths of river valleys.

87 miles – Dunrobin Castle (castle 1030-1230 Mon.-Thu., May, 1030-1730 Mon.-Sat., 1300-1730 Sun., June-Sep., gardens, all year; castle £2.40, child £1.20, gardens free). Home of the dukes of Sutherland, and one of Britain's oldest continuously inhabited houses, the castle is in a beautiful setting overlooking the sea. The old keep in the centre dates from the early 14thC, with substantial additions in c.1650, c.1780 and 1845-50. All the State rooms are open to the public and contain a fascinating display of furniture, art, china, arms, robes and memorabilia, with each room laid out so as to give an insight into the everyday life of the duke and his family in Victorian times. The gardens and grounds are also open to the public and provide a number of attractive walks. Follow the A 9 south through Golspie and across the head of

Loch Fleet by a causeway built by Thomas Telford, the famous Scottish civil engineer, in 1815. The loch is a shallow inlet frequented by many species of wading birds. Turn left on the B 9168.

98 miles – Dornoch. Pop: 1000. Tourist Information (all year), The Square, tel: 086281-0400. A pleasant seaside resort with miles of sandy beaches. Dominating The Square is Dornoch Cathedral, founded in 1224 but much restored through the centuries, most recently in 1924, and still in use. Across the street, part of the old Castle of the Bishops is now incorporated in the Dornoch Castle Hotel. Opposite the Tourist Information office is Dornoch Craft Centre, housed in the old gaol buildings. In addition to the craft shop there is a small museum describing conditions in the gaol two centuries ago (0930-1700 Mon.-Sat., 1200-1700 Sun. summer, 0930-1700 Mon.-Fri. winter; free). Leave Dornoch heading west on the A 949, turning left along the main A 9 for 13 miles to Bonar Bridge (Tourist Information, April-Sep., tel: 08632-333). (Take the A 836 here for Lairg and Loch Shin to join **EXCURSION 6** at Laxford Bridge, midway between Eddrachillis Bay and Durness.) The A 9 goes round the south shore of the Dornoch Firth for 4 miles before you turn right onto the A 836 beyond Fearn Lodge. This road cuts across desolate moorland. Off to the left you may see oil rigs anchored in the Cromarty Firth off Nigg Bay. Rejoin the A 9 heading south.

DETOUR: A faster, though less scenic route from Dornoch is to take the new bridge across the Dornoch Firth. Turn left a few miles out of Dornoch and follow the A 9 through Tain.

Leave the main road at the village of Evanton and turn right on the B 817 to Glenglass to see the impressive Black Rock Ravine.

WALK: 15 min. About 1 mile along the B 817, turn down the third forestry track on your left which is just before a white cottage, and which leads in 200 yd to a rough parking place on the left. From here a footpath leads to a wooden footbridge over the ravine, which is almost invisible until you are on top of it (take great care with small children). The gorge is 200 ft deep, but only 10-11 ft wide, and hung with luxuriant growths of moss and ferns. Turn right on the far side, and the path leads to a second bridge with a more spectacular view which returns you to the track near the parking place. Retrace your route to the main road.

On your right as you drive along is a rounded hill with a large monument on its summit. This is the Fyrish Monument, a replica of an Indian temple gateway erected in 1782 at the behest of a local landowner, in order to ease unemployment in the area. Continue on the A 9, to join the A 862 at a roundabout by a causeway over the Cromarty Firth.

DETOUR: To miss Dingwall and Strathpeffer follow the A 9 into Inverness, crossing the modern Kessock Bridge, built in 1980. A left turn at Tore, on the A 832, leads to Fortrose, where you can visit the interesting remains of 14th-15thC Fortrose Cathedral (all times; free).

135 miles – Dingwall. A royal burgh since 1227 and the county town of Ross-shire. The Town Hall on the High St houses a small museum of local history (0900-1700 Mon.-Sat., May-Sep.; free). Head out of town on the A 834.

139 miles – Strathpeffer. Pop: 1300. Tourist Information (April-Oct.), The Square, tel: 0997-21415. A pretty Victorian spa town. In the pavilion opposite the Tourist Information office are four brass hand-pumps where you can sample the spring waters – very sulphurous and stinking of rotten eggs! Downhill from The Square on the right is Strathpeffer Visitor Centre (1000-1200, 1430-1630; donation), housed in the restored Victorian railway station, with craft shops and a display of turn-of-the-century photographs of the town. Continue on the A 834 and turn right at Contin to reach the Falls of Rogie after a further 2 miles. From a car park on the right there are a number of forest walks centred on the scenic waterfall where salmon can be seen leaping in July and Aug. Backtrack along the A 835, and turn right on the A 832 to Muir of Ord. At Marybank, a minor road on the right leads 22 miles up secluded Strathconan. Muir of Ord has a large distillery offering guided tours (0900-1200, 1400-1600 Mon.-Fri., Feb.-Nov.; free). Turn right on the A 862.

156 miles – Beauly. Pop: 1100. At the end of the wide Main St on the right is the impressive ruin of Beauly Priory, founded c.1230 (HS site, see **Opening Times**; free). From Beauly take the A 862 along the shores of the Beauly Firth, with views across the water to the distant bulk of Ben Wyvis (3433 ft), to reach Inverness (see **A-Z**) (168 miles).

Crail

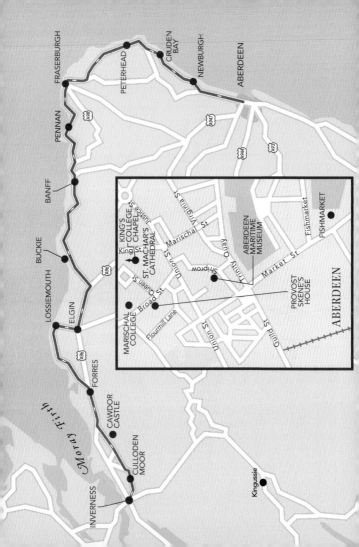

The Northeast Coast

Inverness–Aberdeen. Duration: 2 days.

Head out of Inverness on the B 9006, enjoying the magnificent views across the Moray Firth.

6 miles – Culloden Moor. It was here that Bonnie Prince Charlie's (see **A-Z**) exhausted and half-starved Jacobite army lined up against that of the Duke of Cumberland on 16 April 1746. The Government army was well-equipped and gave no quarter, even putting the wounded and prisoners to the sword. The defeat of the Jacobite army saw the beginnings of nearly a century of military occupation of the Highlands. The Visitor Centre (0900-1830; £1.20, child 60p) explains the events leading up to and including the battle. Just beyond here is the turn-off for Clava Cairns, a large group of Bronze-Age cairns and standing stones 1 mile from the main road. After a further 4 miles turn off for Kilravock Castle and its gardens (conducted tour £1.50). Follow the B 9006 through Croy and past the immense 26-arch viaduct which spans the valley. Carry on east along the same road. In the village of Cephanton, turn right onto the B 9090.

14 miles – Cawdor Castle (1000-1730; £2.40, child £1.30). Despite its associations with Macbeth (see **A-Z**), none of the castle dates back to his time in the mid-11thC. The central tower was built in 1372. The other towers and curtain wall were added in the 14th-16thC. The spiral stair between the old tower and the guardroom is split by a tree. The story goes that a 13thC thane let his horse run loose, deciding that where it stopped he would build his castle. It lay down in the shade of a tree and thus the castle was built around it. Three miles further along the B 9090 becomes the B 9101, joining up with the A 96 at Auldearn, where you turn right.

25 miles – Forres. Pop: 8400. Full services. Tourist Information (Mar.-Oct.), Tolbooth St, tel: 0309-72938. A quiet town amid rich farmland. See the Falconer Museum (0930-1730 Mon.-Fri., 0930-1230, 1330-1750 Sat., 1400-1700 Sun.; free) on Tolbooth St with its fine collection of fossils. There are good views from atop Nelson's Tower. Follow the road east out of Forres, turning off to the left after about 1 mile, onto the B 9011. Turn right at Kinloss onto the B 9089. Follow this road, bearing left towards Burghead, which was once the site of an Iron-Age settlement. The Roman Well, where a spring flows out through the rock, is thought to be an early Christian baptistry. Leaving the coastline, take the B 9012 as far as Duffus Castle (all times; free), a three-storeyed stone keep surrounded by a water-filled moat. Retrace your steps to the B 9040 coast road which passes the Lossiemouth RAF base.

41 miles – Lossiemouth. An attractive coastal town which was the birthplace of Ramsay Macdonald (see **A-Z**). Head south on the A 941.

46 miles – Elgin. Pop: 19,000. Full services. Tourist Information (all year), 17 High St, tel: 0343-542666/543388. A pleasant old town standing in the loops of the River Lossie. The medieval street plan has been preserved, a feature of which were the arcaded passages along the streets. The few that remain have been incorporated into shopfronts, the best example being Braco's Banking House in High St. The fine Museum (1000-1700 Tue.-Fri., 1100-1600 Sat.; £1, child 50p) has local history displays and a collection of fossils. The ruined Cathedral (0930-1900; 60p, child 30p) is a beautiful building, once known as 'The Lantern of the North', which was attacked and burnt in 1390 by the Wolf of Badenoch (see **A-Z**). Go east on the A 96. After 8 miles you will reach the Baxter Visitor Centre (1000-1200, 1300-1600; free), which tells the story of the Baxter family provisions business with the aid of videos and displays. One mile beyond Fochabers, a village which was physically shifted and rebuilt on its present site in 1776 after being 'moved' from nearby Gordon Castle, bear left on the A 98. Continue along this road for 5 miles, then turn left.

61 miles – Buckie. The Maritime Museum (1000-2000 Mon.-Fri., 1000-1200 Sat.; free) houses exhibits of local history and the fishing industry. There's also a superb war memorial. Leaving the town by the same road, turn left onto the A 98 again for 12 miles to Portsoy, which is famed for its Serpentine marble, some of which was used by Louis XIV in the Palace of Versailles.

81 miles – Banff. Pop: 4000. Full services. Tourist Information (Mar.-Oct.), Collie Lodge, tel: 02612-2419. Lying across the River Deveron, Banff is a graceful town, notable for its 18thC architecture. See Duff House (0930-1900 Mon.-Sat., 1400-1900 Sun.; 60p, child 30p), which is said to be modelled on the Villa Borghese in Rome. Continue on the A 98.

82 miles – Macduff. As neighbouring Banff's harbour has silted up, so Macduff has prospered. Its steep streets look across the pleasant estuary. On the hill a 70 ft war memorial affords good views, while an open-air swimming pool cut out of the rocks invigorates. One mile beyond the town, turn left onto the B 9031. After 8 miles a track leads down to Cullykhan Bay, where Troup Head drops some 400 ft to the sea. Along this headland are deep ravines and clefts, and scores of seabirds. Turn left on the B 9031 then down the switchback road to Pennan. Huddling beneath the cliffs that rise above it, this gorgeous little whitewashed village was the location used in the film *Local Hero*. Rejoin the B 9031. At Aberdour beach, half a mile from the main road, a coastal walk of 3 miles runs back to Pennan. There are caves at the eastern edge of this rocky beach and to the west a memorial to Jane Whyte who, in 1884, swam out with a sea line to a ship wrecked offshore, thereby saving the lives of 15 men. Rejoin the B 9031. As you drive along, there are fabulous views along a coastline festooned with dramatic cliffs.

Pennan

Aberdeen

105 miles – Fraserburgh. Pop: 12,500. Tourist Information (Mar.-Oct.), Saltoun Sq., tel: 0346-25315. The town is an important fishing centre, founded by Sir Alexander Fraser in 1546. Follow the A 92 then the A 952 southeast.

122 miles – Peterhead. Pop: 17,000. Full services. Tourist Information (May-Oct.), 54 Broad St, tel: 0779-71904. This pink granite town was founded in 1593. Once the centre of Scotland's whaling industry its large harbour now serves as a gas and oil industry supply base. See the Arbuthnott Museum (1000-1200, 1400-1700 Mon.-Sat.; free) on St. Peter St for local history. Leave the town on the A 952 heading south.

125 miles – Boddam & Buchan Ness. With its 130 ft lighthouse, this is the most easterly point in Scotland. One mile south of here, turn left onto the A 975 and after a further 2 miles turn left for the Bullers of Buchan, 150 ft cliffs above tortured geology where the sea has carved an arch in the rock, allowing waves to crash through.

130 miles – Cruden Bay. There is a fine beach and harbour, and sprawled on cliffs to the north of the village is Slains Castle, said to have been Bram Stoker's inspiration for the setting of *Dracula*.

139 miles – Newburgh. An excellent lunch (particularly the sticky-toffee pudding) can be had at the Udny Arms Hotel in the centre of town and then walked off on the beach which overlooks the immense dunes known as the Sands of Fyvie, where there is a nature reserve with the UK's largest population of eider duck. Continue on the A 975. A mile and a half further south, turn left onto the A 92 which will take you the last 10 miles into Aberdeen (see **A-Z**) (151 miles).

Lerwick

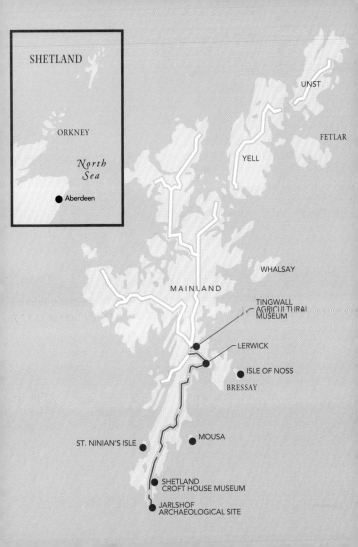

SHETLAND

ORKNEY

North Sea

Aberdeen

UNST

FETLAR

YELL

WHALSAY

MAINLAND

TINGWALL
AGRICULTURAL
MUSEUM

LERWICK

ISLE OF NOSS

BRESSAY

ST. NINIAN'S ISLE

MOUSA

SHETLAND
CROFT HOUSE MUSEUM

JARLSHOF
ARCHAEOLOGICAL SITE

Shetland

Duration: 5 days (inc. ferry journey).

Called Ultima Thule ('The Final Frontier') by the Romans, Shetland remains remote and unvisited, even by Scots from the mainland. Few trees grow here and often the only sounds come from the crash of the sea and the cries of the thousands of seabirds that nest in and around its 900 mile coastline. Its windswept land-scape can be both harshly beautiful and somewhat intimidating. Shetland looks different and indeed is different from the rest of Scotland, having more in common with the Scandinavian coun-tries than the mainland, as the place names illustrate. The islands were ruled by Norsemen for five centuries until 1469, when they were handed over to Scotland as part of a marriage dowry. P&O Scottish Ferries operates an Aberdeen–Lerwick service which takes 14 hr. For details, tel: 0224-572615. Flights to Shetland depart from Glasgow, Edinburgh and Aberdeen air-ports (see **A-Z**). Services are operated by British Airways and Loganair.

Lerwick: Pop: 7,200. Full services. Tourist Information (all year), The Market Cross, tel: 0595-3434. Lerwick is Shetland's main town and its narrow streets and buildings recall its begin-nings as a 17thC fishing port. The Shetland Museum (1000-1900 Mon., Wed. & Fri., 1000-1700 Tue., Thu. & Sat.; free), on Lower Hillhead, chronicles the history of man's settlement on the islands. Fort Charlotte (0930-1900 Mon.-Sat., 1400-1900 Sun.) on the waterfront was first built in 1665 to guard the Sound of Bressay. On the outskirts of town to the south lies the Clickhimin Broch (0930-1900 Mon.-Sat., 1400-1900 Sun.). This fortified Iron-Age fort has a 17 ft-high broch (see **A-Z**) constructed inside it. The Isle of Noss, with its 600 ft cliffs and colonies of auks, gulls and gannets, is 5 miles from Lerwick but can be reached by boat (1000-1700).

SOUTH FROM LERWICK: Take the A 970 to Sandwick (14.5 miles) where you take a boat out to the island of Mousa (0930-1900 Mon.-Sat., 1400-1900 Sun.) whose 40 ft broch is perhaps the best example of a broch tower anywhere in Scotland. Seven miles further south and just off the A 970 is the Shetland Croft House Museum (1000-1300, 1400-1700 Tue.-Sun.; 50p, child 20p), which examines and illustrates the life style of Shetland crofters (farmers) in the 19thC. Continue south to the very tip of the island at Sumburgh (25 miles). Near the modern airport (which is where you will arrive if you fly to Shetland) is the Jarlshof Archaeological Site (0930-1900 Mon.-Sat., 1400-1900 Sun.; £1.20, child 60p). A storm uncovered the remains of these three villages which are believed to have been occupied from the Bronze Age to Viking times. A little further along the coast at Sumburgh Head, puffins can be spotted. Returning to Lerwick it's worth diverting off the A 970 at Boddam to visit St. Ninian's Isle. Linked to the shore by a sand spit, the isle is home to a pre-Norse chapel where Celtic silver was discovered in the 1950s.

NORTH FROM LERWICK: Five miles north of Lerwick, turn off the A 970 at Veensgarth to the Tingwall Agricultural Museum (1000-1300, 1400-1700 Tue., Thu. & Sat., 1000-1300 Wed., 1400-1700 Sun., June-Sep.; 50p, child 20p), which has displays of Shetland crofting life. The rest of northern Shetland and the islands of Whalsay, Yell and Unst can best be explored by car. Take your pick from the many gorgeous secluded beaches and cliffy points covered with seabirds. In the interior peat bogs predominate. Ferries to the outer islands can be booked in advance, tel: 08066-259. Ferries to Whalsay leave from Laxo and for Yell from Toft.

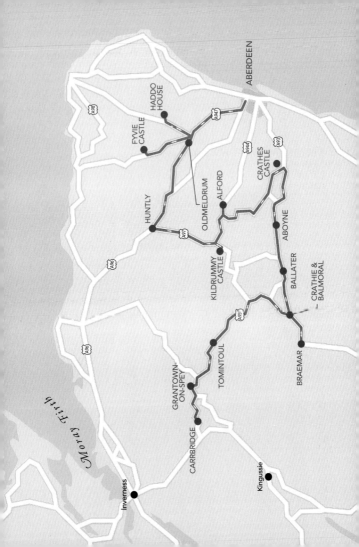

ABERDEEN

HADDO
HOUSE

FYVIE
CASTLE

A96

CRATHES
CASTLE

A944

A93

A947

HUNTLY

OLDMELDRUM

ALFORD

ABOYNE

A96

A97

KILDRUMMY
CASTLE

BALLATER

CRATHIE &
BALMORAL

A97

TOMINTOUL

BRAEMAR

GRANTOWN-
ON-SPEY

A95

CARRBRIDGE

Moray Firth

Inverness

Kingussie

Royal Deeside

Aberdeen–Carrbridge. Duration: 2 days.

Leave Aberdeen on the A 947 for 17 miles through Newmachar to Oldmeldrum.

DETOURS: Follow the A 947 north, turning right onto the B 9170 for 5 miles to Haddo House (1400-1800 May-Sep.; £2, child £1). Designed in 1731 by William Adam, this elegant house is notable for its Adam Revival interior, dating from c.1880, with excellent antique furniture and the two curving stairways to the first-floor balcony. Alternatively, continue on the A 947 for 7 miles to Fyvie Castle (1000-1800; £2, child £1), a grandiose five-towered structure built in the 15thC. Inside, note the great wheeled stair and the plastered ceilings and panelling. It has a fine collection of mid-18thC paintings together with 16thC tapestries and arms.

From Oldmeldrum follow the A 920 and then the A 96.

40 miles – Huntly. Set in wooded parkland half a mile from the pretty 18thC town centre is Huntly Castle (0930-1900 Mon.-Sat., 1400-1900 Sun.; 60p, child 30p). Note the ornamentation above the main door-way and the 15thC dungeon whose walls are scored with ancient graf-fiti. Follow the A 97 south through green, rolling countryside and after 5 miles turn left onto the B 9002 for 2 miles to Leith Hall (1400-1800; £2, child £1). Built c.1650 the mansion is set in 263 acres containing ponds, a bird observation hide, woodland walks, 18thC stables and an ice house. Rejoin the A 97, following it south through Rhynie to Kildrummy Castle (1000-1700; £1, child 20p). It was here that Robert the Bruce (see **A-Z**) sent his wife and her entourage after his defeat at the Battle of Methven. Edward, Prince of Wales, besieged and took the castle only after one Osborne the Smith betrayed the defenders, agree-ing to set fire to it in return for as much gold as he could carry. Bruce's wife was captured and Osborne got his gold, poured molten down his throat! Retrace your route and after 2 miles turn right on the A 944.

58 miles – Alford. Pop: 860. Tourist Information (April-Sep.), Railway Museum, Station Yard, tel: 09755-62052. The village was the scene of a victory against the Covenanters (see **A-Z**) in 1645. Leave on the A 980, signposted Banchory.

63 miles – Craigievar Castle (1400-1800 May-Sep.; £2, child £1). With its gargoyles and turrets this is one of Scotland's best 17thC tower houses. Completed in 1626 it has ceilings painted with religious and mythical figures. A secret stair links the great hall to the roof. Continue on the A 980, turning right at Torphins onto the B 993.

DETOUR: Continue on the A 980 and A 93 for 9 miles to Crathes Castle (castle 1100-1715, gardens 0930-sunset; £3.30, child £1.70), started in 1553 but with 18thC and Queen Anne wings. The spectacular formal gardens have 260-year-old yew hedges, within which each enclosure has a different character and colour scheme from its neighbours.

76 miles – Kincardine o'Neil. Turn right onto the A 93 and follow along what is known as Royal Deeside. Continue through Aboyne, Dinnet and Ballater (Tourist Information, Easter-Oct., Ballater Rd Car Park, tel: 03398-86060).

Balmoral Castle

100 miles – Crathie & Balmoral.
Balmoral (see **A-Z**) is the royal family's Scottish holiday home. The extensive grounds, which stretch away towards Lochnagar, are open to the public (1000-1700 May, June & July; £1.20, child £1: closed when members of the royal family are in residence – watch for the flag). Crathie Church (0930-1730, service 1130 Sun.) is where the royals worship and the south transept is reserved for them. Queen Victoria laid the foundation stone in 1895. Rejoin the A 93 then turn off to the right on the B 976 signposted Tomintoul and the Lecht.

DETOUR: Continue on the A 93 for 9 miles.
Braemar. Tourist Information (Easter-Oct.), Balnellan Rd, tel: 03397-41600. Just before the town see Braemar Castle (1000-1800; £1.20, child 60p), built in 1629. Its star-shaped curtain wall was added by the English after Culloden (see **Bonnie Prince Charlie**) and provided excellent crossfire angles for defence. Also note the pit prison. The Braemar Highland Gathering (see **Events**) is often attended by members of the royal family. Six miles beyond Braemar is the Linn of Dee, the starting point for many fine walks. Return to the B 976. After 5 miles turn left onto the A 939 which goes over the bleak tops past the Lecht Ski Centre.

123 miles – Tomintoul. Tourist Information (Easter-Oct.), The Square, tel: 08074-285. At 1160 ft above sea level, this is the highest village in the Highlands, though not in Scotland, this distinction going to Wanlockhead in the Southern Uplands at an altitude of 1380 ft. From here you can follow the Whisky Trail (see **A-Z**) along the B 9008 visiting eight famous distilleries and returning to Tomintoul. From Tomintoul it is 13 miles to Grantown-on-Spey and a further 9 miles to Carrbridge (see **EXCURSION 11**).

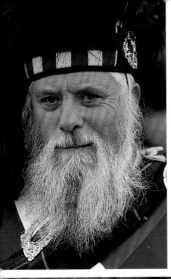

Braemar Highland Gathering

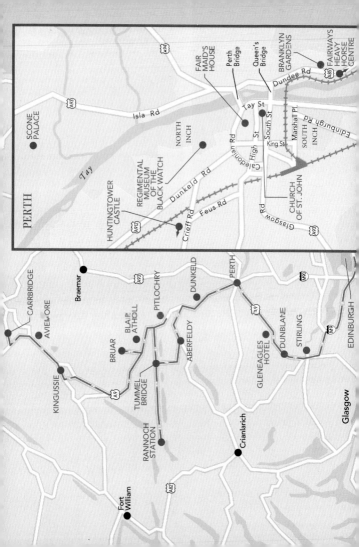

Carrbridge–Edinburgh. Duration: 2-3 days.

Carrbridge can be reached from Aberdeen along the A 944, A 97 and
A 939 (86 miles), and from Inverness on the A 9 and A 938 (25 miles).
Carrbridge. Limited services. Tourist Information (May-Sep.), Main St,
tel: 047984-630. A picturesque bridge built for packhorses in 1717
spans Dulnain Water. Heading south from the town you will encounter
the Landmark Visitor Centre (0930-2030 summer, 0930-1700 winter;
£2.25, child £1.25), which recounts the natural history and history of
the Highlands in its multivision cinema. Outside there's a treetop trail,
maze, balancing trail, pine forest nature centre and adventure playground.

DETOUR: As the B 9153 joins the
A 95, turn left for 2 miles to Boat
of Garten, with the museum and
rolling stock for the Strathspey
Railway (see below). Loch Garten
is 2 miles beyond the village. Until
a pair nested here in 1955 ospreys
were extinct in Scotland. Ospreys
return every year now and can be
viewed from an observation hide
(April-Aug.). Backtrack to the A 95
and then bear left for the B 9152.
6 miles – Aviemore. Pop: 2500.
Full services. Tourist Information
(all year), Grampian Rd, tel: 0479-
810363. This once small village
boomed in the sixties with the
development of the ski slopes in the Cairngorms. It has plenty of pur-
pose-built facilities and accommodation but lacks charm. Carry on
down the road for 2 miles, then turn left for the Strathspey Railway, a
steam railway that runs between Aviemore and Boat of Garten (see
above) (trains run 1200-1700 Sat. & Sun., May-Oct., plus Mon.-Thu.,
July & Aug.). After 1 mile you will come to the Rothiemurchus Visitor
Centre (1000-dusk). This offers ranger services for guided walks, an

exhibition, mountain bike hire, ski hire, a trout farm and clay-pigeon shooting. The ski slopes are 11.5 miles from Aviemore. The chairlift (0900-1630) will carry you almost to the summit of Cairn Gorm and the Ptarmigan Restaurant at 3600 ft. Opposite the visitor centre on your right is the junction with the B 9152. Follow this road and after 1 mile turn left up to Loch an Eilean. This beautiful loch, with a ruined 15thC castle at its centre, is ringed by pine forest. A gentle walk round the loch takes about 45 min. The Visitor Centre here houses an exhibition on the ecology of the area (car park £1). Continue south on the B 970.

15 miles – Feshiebridge. A high, single-arch bridge which spans the River Feshie. Two hundred yards further on there's a road on the left that leads into secluded Glen Feshie. Continue on the B 970 and after almost 1 mile, turn right towards the B 9152. Just beyond the intersection is Loch Insh Water-sports Centre (1000-1800 April-Oct.), offering sailing, windsurfing, canoeing and river expeditions. Follow the road over the Spey at the northern shore of Loch Insh into Kincraig (try the brilliant food at the Ossian Hotel). As you leave the village, turn left onto the B 9152.

18 miles – Highland Wildlife Sanctuary (1000-1700; £7 per car, £3 on foot). A drive-through park that takes you back in time as you see wolf, bear, wildcat, lynx and deer (that all used to live in Scotland) in their natural habitat. The tour takes at least 2.5 hr. Transport can be arranged for those without their own.

21 miles – Kingussie. Pop: 1200. Full services. Tourist Information (May-Sep.), King St, tel: 0540-661297. An attractive town with plenty of accommodation. The Highland Folk Museum (1000-1800 Mon.-Sat., 1400-1800 Sun.; £1.25, child 65p) is excellent.

Outside there are reconstructed dwellings, including a blackhouse from Lewis and a turf-walled house from the central Highlands. Inside, see the dairy, stables and exhibitions of Highland weapons, furniture and music. Also visit the Iona Gallery opposite and Highland China Pottery for crafts. Take the A 86 southwest down the Spey Valley.

23 miles – Newtonmore. Visit the interesting Clan Macpherson Museum (1000-1730 Mon.-Sat., 1430-1730 Sun.) on the Main St, with its clan memorabilia. There is a good golf course and the Highland Games are held on the 1st Sat. in Aug. Leave by the B 9150 to join the A 9 heading south. The road now climbs up over Drumochter Pass, a bleak expanse of scree, heather, glaciated valleys and icy lochs. Keep an eye open for deer. After 29 miles, take a left turn on the B 8079 to Bruar. Follow the footpath up to the Bruar Falls, a trio of waterfalls in a narrow cleft. Return to the road and continue south.

56 miles – Blair Atholl. A pleasant village sitting alongside the River Tilt at the hub of several glens, in an area colonized by Gaels from Ireland in the 5thC: indeed, Atholl means 'New Ireland' in Gaelic. Blair Castle (1000-1800; £2.50, child £1.50, family £7.50) is one of the

premier attractions in Scotland. This white, turretted baronial mansion has parts dating back to 1269 but has been frequently altered. Previous guests include Mary, Queen of Scots (see **A-Z**), Bonnie Prince Charlie (see **A-Z**) and Queen Victoria. Inside, rooms display furniture, china, paintings, arms and armour. Outside, there are a deer park, pony trekking and nature trails. The castle is home to the Duke of Atholl, who commands the only private army in Britain. There is also excellent walking in Glenfender.

59 miles – Pass of Killiecrankie Visitor Centre (0930-1800 June-Aug., 1000-1700 Sep.-May; 20p). The centre tells the story of how, in 1689, the English were defeated by a Jacobite army. In the gorge where the River Garry thunders between rocks, see the Soldier's Leap where one English soldier hurled himself across to escape his pursuers. Just 1 mile beyond the town of Killiecrankie lies Garry Bridge. Turn right at the junction with the B 8079.

DETOUR: Continue on the A 9 for 4 miles.

Pitlochry. Pop: 2600. Full services. Tourist Information (all year), 22 Atholl Rd, tel: 0796-2215/2751. The town lies at the head of the man-made Loch Faskally. The dam and power station are open to the public (0940-1730; £1.50, child 60p) and salmon can be seen through viewing windows on the fish ladder. Pitlochry Festival Theatre, which stages many excellent productions, stands in a modern building on the

banks of the Tay. Other attractions include the Blair Athol Distillery (0900-1700; free) on the south side of town and the colourful Highland Games on the 2nd Sat. in Sep. Retrace your route to the junction of the B 8019 and turn left, heading west.

65 miles – Queen's View. Named after Queen Victoria who visited here in 1866, there are magnificent views down Loch Tummel to Schiehallion (3554 ft). The road towards Kinloch Rannoch runs parallel to Loch Tummel and past Erochty hydro-electric power station.

DETOUR: Take the B 846 along the north shore of Loch Rannoch to Kinloch Rannoch and Rannoch station, beyond the western end of the loch, where the road connects with the West Highland railway line · from Glasgow to Fort William.

Turn left at Tummel Bridge onto the B 846.

85 miles – Braes of Foss. There is a car park here from where you can begin climbs of Schiehallion (see **Walking**). There are stunning views as the road climbs out of the valley. Two miles further on you can turn right on the single-track road signposted Schiehallion which crosses the barren moorland lined with snow posts.

89 miles – Glengoulandie Deer Park (0900-1 hr before sunset; £2 per car, 50p on foot). Herds of red deer, Highland cattle and a variety of endangered species are kept here. Just over half a mile beyond this, on the right, is a road along which you can detour for 3 miles to Fortingall. In the churchyard there is a yew tree reputed to be over 2000 years old, while it is claimed that the nearby Roman fort was the birthplace of Pontius Pilate. Rejoin the B 846. The road shortly begins to widen out.

96 miles – Castle Menzies (1030-1700 Mon.-Sat., 1400-1700 Sun.; £1.50, child 50p). Standing on the right at the foot of Weem Rock, this is a particularly large example of a 16thC Z-plan castle, the design of which allowed for both greater accommodation and improved defences. The castle is currently undergoing restoration but is well

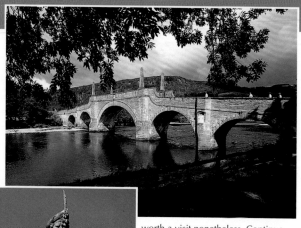

worth a visit nonetheless. Continue on the B 846 to Weem. Weem Hotel is a whitewashed 17thC building. Gen. Wade (see **A-Z**) stayed here on his road- and bridge-building expedition in 1733.

97 miles – Aberfeldy. Pop: 1600. Tourist Information (all year), 8 Dunkeld St, tel: 0887-20276. Beautifully situated on the banks of the Tay, in the centre of the town you will cross the river using the most impressive of Gen. Wade's bridges. Built in 1733 it's the only one still in use in Scotland. Take the A 827 out of Aberfeldy, heading east towards the A 9, through Grandtully and typical Perthshire countryside. After 9 miles you will arrive at Logierait. See the *mortesafes*, to prevent body snatching, and sculpted stones in the churchyard. Join the A 9 heading south. After another 8 miles is The Hermitage, a picturesque area of mixed woodland and rivers with two 18thC follies. A mile-long circular walk takes in the various sights. Continue south on the A 9.

116 miles – Dunkeld. Pop: 600. Full services. Tourist Information (April-Oct.), Main Sq., tel: 0350-2688. Cross Telford's seven-arch bridge into this delightful town, established as one of Scotland's major cathedral towns when some of St. Andrew's relics were brought here for safekeeping because of a fear of Viking coastal raids, and turn left into the old Main Sq. where the Scottish Horse Regiment Museum (1000-1200, 1400-1700 Easter-Sep.; 30p) can be found. In Cathedral St see the restored 'little houses'. Dunkeld Cathedral (0930-1900 Mon.-Sat., 1400-1700 Sun.; free) stands on the banks of the Tay. Though mainly 14th-15thC, parts of it date back to the 12thC. The roof was destroyed in the Reformation (see **A-Z**), but the restored choir is now the parish church. Note the slightly off-centre West Window and the sleeping form of the Wolf of Badenoch (see **A-Z**). Just south of Dunkeld is Birnam Wood, famed in *Macbeth* (see **A-Z**). Rejoin the A 9.

130 miles – Perth (see **A-Z**). Leaving Perth follow the Dunkeld Rd back to the roundabout at Inveralmond. Caithness Glass (0900-1630 Mon.-Fri.), where you can see glass-making in progress, is sited beside it. Tourist Information (April-Oct.), Caithness Glass Car Park, tel: 0738-38481. Follow the A 9 then take the A 823 for half a mile.

145 miles – Gleneagles Hotel. Built in 1924 the hotel is renowned for its championship Kings and Queens golf courses. Despite a reputation for exclusivity the hotel does run more affordable packages, tel: 0764-62231. In nearby Auchterarder see the Great Scots Visitor Centre (1000-1700 June-Aug., 1200-1700 Sep.-May; £1.50, child free) and the last steam-driven textile mill in Scotland at Glenruthven Mill. Rejoin the A 9.

157 miles – Dunblane. Pop: 7000. Full services. Tourist Information (April-Sep.), Stirling Rd, tel: 0786-824428. Dunblane Cathedral (0930-1800 Mon.-Sat., 1400-1800 Sun.) is surrounded by a number of narrow streets with 17th-19thC houses. It dates mainly from the 13thC but has a part-12thC tower. Nearby is the Dean's House, in which can be found the cathedral's museum and library. Follow the A 9/M 9 south.

163 miles – Stirling (see **A-Z**). Take the A 9/M 9 southeast to Edinburgh (see **EDINBURGH**, **A-Z**) (195 miles).

Dunkeld Cathedral

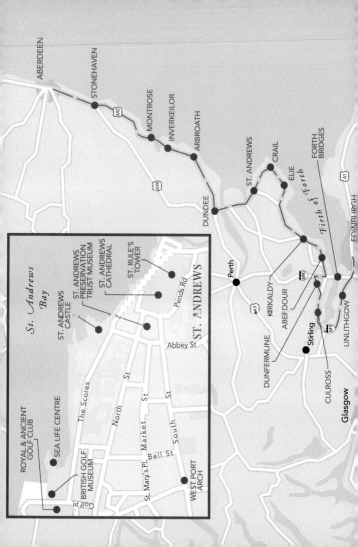

ABERDEEN

STONEHAVEN

MONTROSE

INVERKEILOR

ARBROATH

A92

A94

DUNDEE

ST. ANDREWS

CRAIL

FORTH BRIDGES

ELIE

EDINBURGH

A1

Firth of Forth

Perth

M90

KIRKALDY

ABEFDOUR

A91

DUNFERMLINE

Stirling

M9

LINLITHGOW

CULROSS

Glasgow

St. Andrews Bay

ST. ANDREWS CASTLE

ST. ANDREWS PRESERVATION TRUST MUSEUM

ST. ANDREWS CATHEDRAL

ST. RULE'S TOWER

Pends Rd

ST. ANDREWS

Abbey St

ROYAL & ANCIENT GOLF CLUB

SEA LIFE CENTRE

The Scores

North St

Market St

South St

Bell St

St. Mary's Pl.

BRITISH GOLF MUSEUM

Golf Pl.

WEST PORT ARCH

Aberdeen–Edinburgh. Duration: 3-4 days.

Leave Aberdeen heading south on the A 92.

15 miles – Stonehaven. Pop: 9000. Full services. Tourist Information (Easter-Sep.), The Square, tel: 0569-62806. New Stonehaven, established in the 19thC, stands above the rather more interesting Old Stonehaven which clusters around the harbour and is the site of the Tolbooth (1000-1200, 1400-1700 Mon. & Thu.-Sat., 1400-1700 Wed., June-Sep.; free), built in the late 16thC as a storehouse. However, in the 18thC it was used as a prison for the Episcopal clergy and nowadays is a museum with displays on local history and the fishing industry. Continue south on the A 92.

17 miles – Dunnottar Castle (0900-1800, last entry 1700, Mon.-Fri., 1400-1700 Sun.; £1, child 50p). The present ruins date from 1392, with a huge gatehouse added in 1575, and are situated on a dramatic rocky outcrop with sheer cliffs to the sea. The castle has witnessed a number of actions over the centuries, notably in 1651 when English troops besieged it for eight months in an unsuccessful attempt to wrest the Scottish regalia and State papers, and in 1685 when nearly 170 Covenanters (see **A-Z**) were imprisoned in the castle dungeon, with the result that many of them died. Dunnottar recently appeared in the guise of Elsinore in Zeffirelli's film of *Hamlet*. Follow the A 92 south along the coast through Inverbervie and the former fishing villages of Gourdon and Johnshaven.

37 miles – Montrose. Pop: 10,000. Full services. Tourist Information (April-Sep.), 212 High St, tel: 0674-72000. The town lies at the mouth of the South Esk beside the Montrose Basin, now a reserve for migrating birds. The Museum and Art Gallery (1030-1300, 1400-1700; free) in Panmure Pl. has geology and whaling displays, while the William Lamb Memorial Studio (1400-1700 Sun., July & Aug.; free) exhibits works by this local sculptor and etcher who died in 1951.

45 miles – Inverkeilor. Turn left for 1 mile down to Lunans Bay with its remarkable 'singing sands', the Red Castle at its centre and the 250 ft cliff of Red Head at the south end. Semiprecious stones can be found at Boddin Point to the north. Rejoin the A 92.

53 miles – Arbroath. Pop: 24,000. Full services. Tourist Information (all year), Market Pl., tel: 0241-72609/76680. Arbroath Abbey (0930-1900 Mon.-Sat., 1400-1900 Sun.; 60p, child 30p) was completed in 1214, having been founded by William the Lion and dedicated to St. Thomas à Becket. Built of sandstone it has fine vaulted structures both in the sacristy beside the transept and in the Abbot's House. Also see the Signal Tower Museum (1030-1300, 1400-1700; free), which was the land base for the Bell Rock lighthouse and now recounts local history. Continue on the A 92. At Muirdrum, 6 miles on, turn left.

61 miles – Carnoustie. Full services. Tourist Information (April-Sep.), The Library, High St, tel: 0241-52258. The town has a renowned links golf course. Follow the A 930 through Broughty Ferry.

72 miles – Dundee (see **A-Z**). At this point you can take the A 85 to Perth (see **EXCURSION 11**), 22 miles to the west. However, the main route follows the A 92 which spans the 1.5 mile-wide Firth of Tay into Fife. The railway bridge and the legs of the older version which collapsed in 1879 as a train was crossing, killing 75 people, can be seen further up the estuary. Go south on the A 92, turning left at Carrick onto the A 919.

77 miles – Leuchars. Turn left at the roundabout on the east side of the town for the 12thC church topped by an unusual 17thC bell tower, which displays some of the best Norman architecture in Britain. One mile on from the church lies Earlshall Castle (1400-1800; £2.50, child £1) set in wooded grounds. Built in 1546 by Sir William Bruce, its long gallery has fabulously painted ceilings of coats of arms and mythological beasts. There's an interesting collection of Scottish weaponry, and in the attractive gardens topiary yews shaped as chessmen. Leave by the A 919, turning left onto the A 91.

83 miles – St. Andrews (see **A-Z**). Take the A 917, heading towards the East Neuk fishing villages.

92 miles – Crail. Full services. Tourist Information (June-Sep.), Museum and Heritage Centre, Marketgate, tel: 0333-50869. Once a major trading port with the Continent, Crail's quaint old streets lead down to the stunningly pretty harbour, crowded by red-roofed houses and a stonewall waterfront. There are fine views out to the Isle of May, a reserve whose rugged cliffs are inhabited by puffins, guillemots and razorbills. It was once home to Benedictine monks and can be reached

Isle of May

by a 40 min boat journey from Crail or Anstruther (see below). You can buy freshly cooked lobster and crabs at the harbour, and for excellent food try the Crail Inn. Leave the town southwest on the A 917.

96 miles – Anstruther. Tourist Information (Easter-Sep.), St. Ayles, tel 0333-311073. Another delightful fishing village, with old merchants' houses lining the harbour. The Scottish Fisheries Museum (1000-1730 Mon.-Sat., 1100-1700 Sun.; £1, child 50p) on the harbour covers the history of the fishing industry in Scotland from whaling to salmon fishing. Also in the harbour you can board the North Carr Lightship (1000-1700; 50p, child 30p), now a museum.

98 miles – Pittenweem. The narrow streets and houses with Flemish gables all lead down to the harbour that's home to the East Neuk fishing fleet. Along from the harbour is St. Fillian's Cave (*weem* means 'cave' in Pictish – see **Picts**) which was used as a retreat in the 12thC by monks from the Isle of May and which gave the town its name (Place of the Cave).

DETOUR: A few hundred yards east of Pittenweem centre a road turns off to the right to Kellie Castle (castle 1400-1800, grounds 1000-sunset; £2.80, child £1.40), just over 3 miles away. It's present T-shape was

designed in the 16thC though parts of the castle date back to 1360. Set in 4 acres of grounds overlooking the Firth of Forth it was home to the Oliphant family for 250 years and has interesting plasterwork and painted panelling. Turn back to the main road.

100 miles – St. Monans. The village clings to the rocky shore and the pretty harbour, cottages and St. Monans Church (with a model sailboat hanging from the transept) all make it worth a visit.

102 miles – Elie. Full services. This attractive town is very popular, with its harbour, golf course and peaceful atmosphere. From the town there is a 4 mile coastal walk to Lower Largo (see below) on Largo Bay. The road bends inland, away from the coast. Follow it to its junction with the A 915 and turn left. A few hundred yards beyond the junction is the turn-off for Lower Largo. Follow this road for half a mile.

106 miles – Lower Largo. Alexander Selkirk, on whom Daniel Defoe based Robinson Crusoe, was born here. Selkirk had run away to sea but was abandoned on the island of Juan Fernandez in 1705 for rebelling against the ship's captain. He was rescued four years later. Retrace your steps to the main road. At Leven, turn left off the A 915 onto the A 955 which passes through Methil and Buckhaven, along the coast.

St. Monans

116 miles – Ravenscraig Castle (0930-1900 Mon.-Sat., 1400-1900 Sun.; 60p, child 30p). This striking 15thC ruin sits on a rocky knoll in parkland between Dysart and Kirkcaldy. It was one of the first castles in the UK to be designed for defence against artillery.

117 miles – Kirkcaldy. Pop: 46,000. Full services. Tourist Information (all year), Esplanade, tel: 0592-267775. The birthplace of Adam Smith (see **A-Z**). Follow the A 921 out of town, passing Kinghorn and Burntisland.

125 miles – Aberdour. A popular resort because of its Silver Sands beach and proximity to Edinburgh. You can get boats out to Inchcolm Island and Abbey from here. The abbey was founded in gratitude for Alexander I's deliverance after he was driven onto the island's rocks in a storm. Leave the A 921 4 miles beyond Aberdour to join the M 90 at Junction 1, heading north. Leave the motorway to the left at Junction 3 to take the A 907 west to Dunfermline.

136 miles – Dunfermline (see **A-Z**). Take the A 994, passing Crossford and Cairneyhill, then take the B 9037 at the roundabout where the road joins the A 985. At High Valleyfield, follow the minor coastal road down to Culross.

143 miles – Culross (pronounced 'Kew-ross'). This restored medieval village has changed little over the centuries. The Town House (1100-1300, 1400-1700 Mon.-Sat., 1400-1700 Sun.; £1, child 50p) was built in 1526 and combined roles as the council chambers and prison (with criminals held on the ground floor, witches in the attic). The village is protected by order of the Secretary of State for Scotland, and when the electricity board wanted to build a sub-station in the village, it was housed inside a copy of a local cottage so as not to spoil the look and atmosphere of the surrounding area! You can walk up cobbled streets to see the 13thC Cistercian abbey and the palace. Past the abbey follow the road until it intersects with the A 895 and turn left.

147 miles – Kincardine. Tourist Information (Easter-Sep.), Pine 'n' Oak, Kincardine Bridge Rd, tel: 0324-83422. Cross Kincardine Bridge (A 876) with good views up and down the Forth. Continue along the same road until it becomes the M 876, leaving that motorway at Junction 7 to go onto the M 9 heading for Edinburgh. Leave the M 9 at Junction 4, taking the A 803 east.

160 miles – Linlithgow. Pop: 9500. Full services. Tourist Information (all year), Burgh Halls, The Cross, tel: 0506-844600. Linlithgow Palace (0930-1900 Mon.-Sat., 1400-1700 Sun.; £1, child 50p) is on the left in the centre of town. A royal manor house existed here from the 12thC, though the original was burnt down in 1424 and the present palace was reconstructed over the following two centuries. Mary, Queen of Scots (see **A-Z**) was born here in 1542. The church of St. Michael was enclosed within the castle walls by Edward I in 1302 and later the English garrison used it as a storehouse. It too was burnt down in 1424 and had to be reconstructed. As you leave the town, take the A 706 north.

163 miles – Bo'ness. Full services. Tourist Information (May-Aug.), Hamilton's Cottage, Bo'ness Station, tel: 0506-826626. The present name is a contraction of Borrowstounness. Kinneil House (0900-1900 Mon.-Sat., 1400-1900 Sun.; 60p), seat of the dukes of Hamilton, stands 1 mile west of Bo'ness. This fine 16th and 17thC house has beautiful wall paintings and decorated ceilings. James Watt developed his steam engine in an outhouse in the grounds. In the house's converted stables is Kinneil Museum, telling the estate's history, and next to it is a Roman fort which formed part of the Antonine Wall (see **A-Z**). The town is also the home of the Scottish Railway Preservation Society. Leave Bo'ness by the A 993 heading east. At its junction with the A 904, turn right and rejoin the M 9 at Junction 3. At Junction 1 follow the A 8000 for 2 miles. The Forth Bridge Visitor Centre (0900-1900), between the bridges, details the history of Forth crossings (see **Forth Road & Rail Bridges**). Also worth a visit is Dalmeny House (0900-1300, 1400-1900;

£1.80, child £1.20) in nearby Dalmeny. Designed in 1815 this Tudor Gothic mansion is noted for its collection of 18thC British pictures and the Napoleon Room with his French furniture contrasting with the simple chair and desk from St. Helena. Two miles west of South Queensferry lies the impressive Hopetoun House (1000-1730; house & grounds £2.80, child £1.40, grounds only £1.50, child 50p). Redesigned and enlarged by William Adam, it was completed in 1767. Containing much of the original furniture, it also houses paintings by Gainsborough, Raeburn and Canaletto. There's a family museum, and extensive grounds with a deer park, walled garden, and woodland and coastal walks.

175 miles – Ingliston. Turn off right to Ratho almost immediately after joining the A 8. Here can be found the Edinburgh Canal Centre, telling the story of the Union Canal which stretches to Falkirk to join the Forth and Clyde Canal. You can take cruises, hire rowing boats or just watch and relax in the comfort of the Bridge Inn or Pop Inn. Rejoin the A 8 for 7 miles into Edinburgh (see **EDINBURGH, A-Z**) (182 miles)

Pitlochry Dam

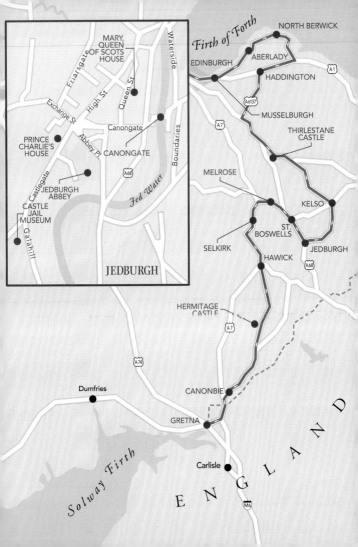

NORTH BERWICK

Firth of Forth

A1

ABERLADY

EDINBURGH

HADDINGTON

A6137

MUSSELBURGH

A7

THIRLESTANE
CASTLE

MELROSE

KELSO

ST.
BOSWELLS

SELKIRK

JEDBURGH

A68

HAWICK

HERMITAGE
CASTLE

A7

A74

Dumfries

CANONBIE

GRETNA

Solway Firth

Carlisle

E N G L A N D

M6

JEDBURGH inset

MARY,
QUEEN
OF SCOTS
HOUSE

Waterside

Friarsgate

Exchange St.

High St.

Queen St.

Canongate

CANONGATE

PRINCE
CHARLIE'S
HOUSE

Abbey Pl.

A68

Boundaries

Jed Water

Castlegate

JEDBURGH
ABBEY

CASTLE
JAIL
MUSEUM

Galahill

JEDBURGH

Edinburgh–Gretna Green. Duration: 3 days.

Leave Edinburgh on the A 1 and join the A 199 signposted
Musselburgh.

5 miles – Musselburgh. Pop: 19,000. Full services. Tourist Information
(June-Sep.), Brunton Hall, tel: 031-6656597. The 17thC Pinkie House
(1400-1700 Tue.) in Loretto School has a fine painted gallery and plasterwork ceilings. The waterfront beside the 16thC Esk Bridge is a peaceful and pleasant respite from the bustle of the rest of the town. Follow
the A 199 past Musselburgh Racecourse and join the B 1348.

8 miles – Scottish Mining Museum (1000-1630 Tue.-Fri., 1200-1700
Sat. & Sun.; free). On the site of an old colliery, this museum displays
800 years of mining history with audio-visual displays and exhibitions.
Follow the B 1348 through Prestonpans, Cockenzie and Port Seton,
past the immense power station to join the A 198.

14 miles – Gosford House (1400-1700 Wed., Sat. & Sun.; £1, child
50p). A combined design, the central part of this house overlooking the
Forth is by Robert Adam (see **A-Z**) and the wings by William Young. It
has an impressive marble hall and attractive gardens.

15 miles – Aberlady. There's a fine old church here and the bay is a
nature reserve with many species of birds. Continue on the A 198.
Three miles further on is Gullane, which has good golf courses on
either side of the road as you enter the village, including the Muirfield
championship course. After 2 miles turn left into Dirleton. The beautiful
ruins of Dirleton Castle (0930-1900 Mon.-Sat., 1400-1900 Sun.; £1,
child 50p) date back to 1225, and its delightful gardens and 17thC
bowling green are enclosed by a complete wall. Continue through this
attractive village to rejoin the A 198.

22 miles – North Berwick. Pop: 5400. Full services. Tourist
Information (all year), Quality St, tel: 0620-2197. A traditional resort on
the shores of the Forth. Set in the rocks beside the pleasant harbour is a
heated open-air pool, while the Museum (1000-1300, 1400-1700
Mon.-Sat., 1400-1700 Sun.; free), recounting local history, is to be
found on School St. The Bass Rock lies offshore. This 350 ft island with
its thousands of seabirds can be reached by boat: details from the
Tourist Information office.

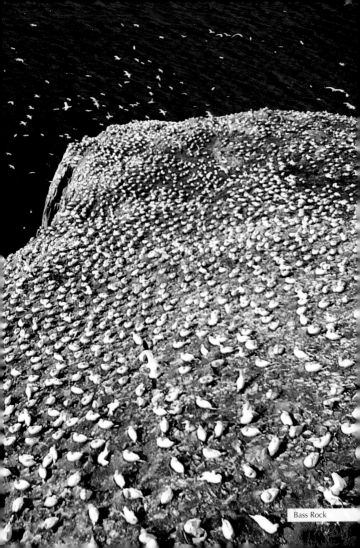

Bass Rock

Leaving town on the A 198 you pass Berwick Law, 613 ft of volcanic rock topped by a Napoleonic watchtower and a whalebone archway, which offers wonderful views across the firth.

26 miles – Tantallon Castle (0930-1900 Mon.-Sat., 1400-1900 Sun.; £1, child 50p). Sitting on shoreline cliffs, its walls and towers intact, the castle was built in 1375 and finally destroyed by Gen. Monk in 1651. Rejoin the A 198. After 5 miles turn right on the A 1 and after a further 3 miles turn left.

35 miles – Hailes Castle (0930-1900 Mon.-Sat., 1400-1900 Sun.; 60p, child 30p). Bothwell brought Mary, Queen of Scots (see **A-Z**) to this 13thC castle after having to flee his family home in 1567. Rejoin the A 1.

38 miles – Haddington. This well-preserved town retains its medieval street plan and contains nearly 300 buildings of historical or architectural interest. St. Mary's Church (1000-1600 Mon.-Sat., 1300-1600 Sun.), where John Knox (see **A-Z**) worshipped as a boy, is an impressive building on the banks of the River Tyne. Across the river is the Waterside Bistro (try the deep-fried Brie and the steak and Guinness pie). Nearby is Lennoxlove House (1400-1700 Wed., Sat. & Sun.; £2, child £1), named in memory of the love the Duchess of Lennox had for

her husband, which has a fine collection of porcelain, portraits and furniture together with gardens. Leave Haddington on the A 6137, cross the B 6355 and continue on the A 6137. After 8 miles turn sharp right to the delightful Humbie Parish Church set in a wooded dell. Rejoin the A 6137 and continue through Humbie. Turn left on the A 68, the road climbing Soutra Hill and offering panoramic views back to Edinburgh. One mile beyond Lauder turn left onto the A 697 signposted Kelso and Coldstream.

59 miles – Thirlestane Castle (castle 1400-1700, grounds 1200-1800, Wed., Thu. & Sun., May, June & Sep.; Sun.-Fri., July & Aug.; £2.50, child £2). The redstone, spired home of the Maitland family. Set on a mound surrounded by trees and parkland it has marvellous 17thC State rooms. Turn left out of the castle grounds onto the A 697. Continue for 3.5 miles then turn right and join the A 6089 signposted Gordon and Kelso. Travel through Gordon, and 3 miles beyond, turn right for 1 mile to Mellerstain House (1230-1630 Sun.-Fri.). Built in the 1720s this beautiful Georgian mansion has a superb collection of paintings (Constable, Gainsborough and Veronese) and furniture (Chippendale, Sheraton and Hepplewhite). The house is surrounded by parkland with terraced gardens to the rear. Rejoin the A 6089. There are fabulous views to the west across the Borders.

76 miles – Kelso. Pop: 5600. Full services. Tourist Information (April-Oct.), Turret House, tel: 0573-23464. Kelso is a delightful town with its expansive square and cobbled streets. See Kelso Abbey (0930-1900 Mon.-Sat., 1400-1900 Sun.; free), built in 1128, the oldest and most grandiose of the Border abbeys. It was razed by the Earl of Hertford in 1545. Floors Castle (1030-1730 Sun.-Thu., all week July & Aug.; £2.20, child £1.80) was designed by William Adam in 1821 and is the seat of the Duke of Roxburgh. This striking mansion with its ballustraded and towered roof contains 17th-18thC French furniture and a collection of Chinese and Dresden porcelain. Set in magnificent parkland overlooking the River Tweed, it's a 'must' for any visitor. Leave Kelso on the A 698, crossing Rennie's Bridge with its five arches and columns, modelled on London Bridge by John Rennie (see **A-Z**) in 1800. Travel through Heiton and Crailing on the A 698 for 7.5 miles to the junction with the A 68, and turn right.

Floors Castle

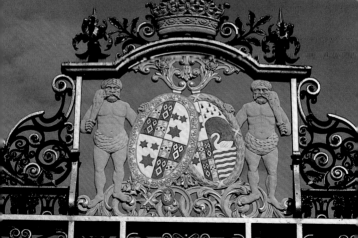

85 miles – Jedburgh. Pop: 4000. Full services. Tourist Information (all year), Murray's Green, tel: 0835-63435/63688. The home of the most intact of the Border abbeys. This Augustinian priory (0930-1900 Mon.-Sat., 1400-1900 Sun.; £1, child 50p), with its complete wheel window and sculpted Norman doorway, was partially destroyed eight times before finally being abandoned in 1545. Mary, Queen of Scots House (1000-1700; 75p, child 50p) on Queen St, not surprisingly accommodated the queen after she had ridden to Hermitage Castle (see page 169) to see the Earl of Bothwell in 1566, a journey that nearly killed her. It is now a visitor centre detailing her life. Also worth seeing are Prince Charlie's House (Castlegate), the Castle Jail with its museum of local history (1000-1200, 1300-1700; 50p, child 25p) and the Canongate, the 16thC arched bridge that used to form the main entrance to the town. Take the A 68 north signposted Melrose.

95 miles – St. Boswells. The village has an attractive tree-lined green. Turn right onto the B 6404 into the village and follow the road for 1.5 miles to the turn-off to Dryburgh Abbey on the B 6356.

98 miles – Dryburgh Abbey (0930-1900 Mon.-Sat., 1400-1900 Sun.; £1.20, child 60p). Founded in the 12thC, the abbey is idyllically set in parkland. Sir Walter Scott (see **A-Z**) is buried in the church. Backtrack along the B 6356 and turn left, signposted Scott's View. The road climbs steeply up Bemersyde Hill.

100 miles – Scott's View. Fabulous views are afforded over the Tweed to the three peaks of the Eildon Hills. This was Scott's favourite view and it's said that on his death the hearse, pulled by his own horses, stopped here automatically on its way to the abbey. Immediately below, where the Tweed almost loops back on itself, is the site of the original Mailros monastery that gives the nearby town its name. Continue on the B 6356 through lush, green countryside for three-quarters of a mile, turning left onto the B 360.

104 miles – Melrose. Pop: 2200. Full services. Tourist Information (April-Oct.), Priorwood Gardens, tel: 0896-822553. A small but pretty town standing at the foot of the Eildon Hills and on the banks of the Tweed. Melrose Abbey (0930-1900 Mon.-Sat., 1400-1900 Sun.; £1, child 50p), built in 1136, is the true heart of the town. Although repeatedly destroyed by the English, much of this Cistercian abbey remains.

Its beautifully carved stonework is noted particularly for its gargoyles and, somewhat mysteriously, the figure of a pig playing the bagpipes! Robert the Bruce's (see **A-Z**) heart is buried somewhere in the abbey. The Abbey Museum (across Cloisters Rd) contains relics from the abbey and the Trimontium Roman fort in the Eildon Hills. There are pleasant walks both across the suspension bridge over the Tweed to the lovely village of Gattonside and up into the Eildon Hills (the latter, signposted from the square in Melrose, are approximately 4 miles). Follow the A 6091 out of town for 2.5 miles and at a large roundabout take the first exit onto the B 6360 signposted Abbotsford House.

107 miles – Abbotsford House (1000-1700 Mon.-Sat., 1400-1700 Sun.; £1.60, child 80p). Built in 1822 and designed by Sir Walter Scott, Abbotsford was his home until his death in 1832. Scott wrote many of his most famous books, including *Rob Roy* and *Heart of Midlothian*, here. A collector of historical relics, he amassed arms and armour (notably Rob Roy's gun and Bonnie Prince Charlie's quaich, a small drinking cup), together with over 9000 rare books. These remain on view. There are extensive gardens. Continue on the B 6360, turning after 2 miles on the A 7 for Selkirk. The road runs along an attractive valley bottom.

112 miles – Selkirk. Pop: 5400. Full services. Tourist Information (April-Oct.), Halliwell's House, tel: 0750-20054. The town sits on the hillside overlooking the woollen mills down by the river. Halliwell's House Museum (1000-1700 Mon.-Sat., 1400-1600 Sun.; 60p, child 30p), in a row of 18thC buildings, details the town's history and has a fine collection of old ironmongery. In Market Pl., outside the court-house, is a statue of Sir Walter Scott. You can visit his courtroom with his bench and chair by application to the district council (1400-1600 July & Aug., tel: 0750-20096). Near the river visit Selkirk Glass (0900-1230, 1330-1700 Mon.-Thu., 0900-1200 Fri.) to see glass being made. Take the A 7 south from the town, offering wonderful views across the Border hills.

123 miles – Hawick. Pop: 16,300. Full services. Tourist Information (April-Oct.), Common Haugh, tel: 0450-72547. Hawick is very much a market town and is the primary centre for knitwear in Scotland. Hawick Museum (1000-1200, 1300-1700 Mon.-Sat., 1400-1700 Sun.; 50p, child 25p), in Wilton Park Lodge, has a good collection of Border arte-facts, especially relating to knitwear. There are also pleasant walks along the banks of the River Teviot. Hawick is probably the best place to buy woollens in the Borders. Take the B 6399 from the centre of Hawick heading south. This narrow, windy road leads through a land-scape of pasture, forests and bald, grassy peaks.

138 miles – Hermitage Castle (0930-1900 Mon.-Sat., 1400-1900 Sun.; 60p, child 30p). This dour 13thC Border castle is in fantastic condition. Its H-shaped outer wall must have looked very similar when Mary, Queen of Scots made her 50 mile round trip from Jedburgh to visit the wounded Earl of Bothwell here in 1566. The castle has a violent history of Border skirmishes; indeed, one member of the de Soulis family (its early owners) is reputed to have been encased in lead and boiled alive in a cauldron! Continue on the B 6399 and then the B 6357.

151 miles – Canonbie. A pretty little village. The Riverside Inn serves delicious food. Join the A 7, turning south. Cross briefly into England and 5 miles further on turn right onto the A 6071 just north of Longtown. Follow the A 6071 for 4 miles and join the A 74 heading north. Alternatively, you could start **EXCURSION 1** at Gretna Green and continue through Dumfries and Galloway back to Glasgow.

Aberdeen

ABE

Aberdeen: Pop: 214,000. Tourist Information (all year), St. Nicholas House, Broad St, tel: 0224-632727. Hemmed in by the River Dee to the south and the Don to the north, the 'Granite City' is the capital of the northeast, dating back to 1179. Aberdeen, meaning 'mouth of the Don', is the UK's third-largest fishing port, but it was the discovery of oil in the North Sea which brought real prosperity to the city as the oil companies and their attendant personnel flocked into the area. Today it is the price of a barrel of crude, rather than the catches of cod and herring, that determines the city's fortunes.

Along the cobbled High St of the Old Town (to the north of the present city centre) lie King's College Chapel and, across Machar Dr, St. Machar's Cathedral (0800-1700 Mon.-Sat., 1400-1700 Sun.). The chapel was built in 1494, and its crown spire is similar to that on St. Giles' Cathedral (see **EDINBURGH-WALK**). St. Machar's was founded in 1131 but was destroyed by the Wolf of Badenoch (see **A-Z**), and rebuilt in 1424. Apart from the sandstone towers it is built almost entirely of local granite. On Broad St, in the city centre, is the impressive façade of Marischal College, the second-largest granite building in Europe, founded in 1593. Built on lands taken from the Catholic Church during the Reformation (see **A-Z**), the college was intended as a Protestant alternative to the 'Papist' university at King's College. Today it is part of Aberdeen University, and contains an anthropological museum (1000-1900 Mon.-Sat., 1400-1700 Sun.; free). Across the road is Provost Skene's House (1000-1700; free), the oldest dwelling-place in the city, housing a museum of civic life. Provost Ross's House on Shiprow contains the Aberdeen Maritime Museum (1000-1700; free), which records the history of the fishing, shipbuilding and oil industries in the region. Nearby, along Market St, is the Fishmarket, Scotland's largest, where the fishing fleet is unloaded and the catch sold. It is a fascinating spectacle, but you have to be up early to enjoy it – auctioning begins at 0730. See **EXCURSIONS 10 & 12**.

Accidents & Breakdowns: If you are involved in an accident where no one has been hurt, exchange name, address and insurance details with the other driver, and take the names and addresses of any witnesses. Inform your insurance company or car rental firm as soon as possible. If there are any injuries, an ambulance should be called and the police must be informed. In the event of a breakdown, there are emergency telephones at regular intervals along motorways and major roads. In remote areas you may have to seek help from the nearest farm or village. Visitors who are members of motoring organizations belonging to the International Touring Alliance can summon assistance free of charge from the Automobile Association (24 hr breakdown service, tel: 041-8123999), or the Royal Automobile Club (24 hr rescue service, tel: 041-2485474). See **Consulates**, **Driving**, **Emergency Numbers**.

Accommodation: Scotland offers a huge range of holiday accommodation, from self-catering cottages to luxury hotels. Hotels range from intimate, family-run establishments to romantic castles and country houses, while the ubiquitous 'bed and breakfast' offers excellent value. The B&B is usually a private home where you can rent a bedroom from as little as £8-10 per night. The bathroom is shared, and a hearty cooked breakfast is included in the price. A hotel room with a bath will cost around £30-75 per night, while self-catering accommodation (usually booked in advance) ranges from £60-250 per week, depending on size and degree of luxury. The Scottish Tourist Board (STB) has recently introduced a two-tier system for classifying hotels and guesthouses: the range of facilities provided by an establishment is indicated by the Classification, from one crown for basic accommodation to five crowns for a luxury suite; and the quality of service is shown by the Quality grading, which can be Approved, Commended or Highly Commended. Hotel room prices must, by law, be prominently displayed. Regional lists of hotel, guesthouse, bed and breakfast, and self-catering accommodation can be obtained free from the STB (see **Tourist Information**). Also available from the STB and from bookshops are the following guides: *Scotland: Where to Stay, Hotels and Guesthouses* (£5.90); *Scotland: Where to Stay, Bed and Breakfast* (£3.90); and *Scotland: Self-Catering Accommodation* (£5.30). Advance booking of accommodation is recommended for the Easter weekend and during July and Aug. The STB runs a free local booking service called Book-a-Bed-Ahead. Simply call at any STB Tourist Information office and they will reserve a room for you anywhere in Scotland. A small deposit will be charged, but this will be deducted from your hotel bill. See **Camping & Caravanning**, **Youth Hostels**.

Adam, Robert (1728-92): Robert Adam was one of 18thC Britain's most famous architects. After four years' study in Rome he returned to lead a neoclassical movement which laid as much importance on a building's interior as on its exterior appearance. He was renowned for the detail of his architectural designs; one of his best-known works is the classical façade on the north side of Charlotte Sq. in Edinburgh. Towards the end of his life he moved from classical forms to romantic designs, the most famous of which is Culzean Castle (see **EXCURSION 1**).

Airports: Scotland has four principal airports: Glasgow, Edinburgh, Prestwick and Aberdeen. Regular shuttle services run from London to Glasgow, Edinburgh and Aberdeen, while transatlantic flights land at Prestwick and Glasgow. British Airways and Loganair have many internal flights connecting the main cities to smaller outlying airfields. All four airports have modern terminals with tourist information, accommodation, bank, currency exchange, post office, restaurants and shops. Glasgow Airport is 9 miles west of the city centre, 15-20 min by bus or taxi. Prestwick Airport is about 31 miles south of Glasgow, 1 hr away by bus or train, and about 80 miles from Edinburgh, 2 hr by bus. Edinburgh Airport is 6 miles west of the city centre, about 30 min by bus or taxi. Aberdeen Airport is 7 miles northwest of the city centre, 30 min by bus or taxi. British Airways offers a special Highland Rover ticket. This costs £213 and permits eight flights within a period of 8-21 days among the following airports: Glasgow, Edinburgh, Aberdeen, Inverness, Benbecula, Stornoway, Wick, Kirkwall (Orkney) and Lerwick (Shetland). It must be purchased at least seven days in advance. For further information from British Airways, tel: 0345-222111.
Flight information: Aberdeen, tel: 0224-722331; Edinburgh, tel: 031-3331000; Glasgow, tel: 041-8871111; Prestwick, tel: 0292-79822.

Barra Airport

Antonine Wall: This Roman rampart of turf and stone was built around AD 142 at the order of Emperor Antoninus Pius, to ward off the invading Picts (see **A-Z**). It took the legionnaires three years to build the turfed stone wall, defended by forts every 2 miles, and another 30 years to decide to abandon it in the face of relentless assaults. It marks the northernmost extent of the Roman Empire in Britain, and runs between Old Kilpatrick on the Clyde and Bridgeness on the Firth of Forth, 40 miles away. There were 19 forts, the best preserved of which can be seen at Rough Castle, near Bonnybridge, a few miles west of Falkirk. Rough Castle is under the care of the National Trust for Scotland (see **A-Z**). See **EXCURSION 12**.

Arran: Pop: 3450. Tourist Information (all year), The Pier, Brodick, tel: 0770-2140, and Lochranza, tel: 077083-320. Arran is a large island (20 miles by 11 miles) lying in the Firth of Clyde. It can be reached by car ferry from Ardrossan in Ayrshire, or from Claonaig (see **EXCURSION 4**) in Argyllshire. The northern half of the island is mountainous, and provides good hill walking and rock climbing. The highest point is Goat Fell (2866 ft), reached by a footpath beginning at the bridge over the Glen Rosa Water, about 1 mile north of Brodick (see **Walking**). The rest of Arran offers less strenuous walking, good sea angling and a number of prehistoric sites, and there is much to interest the naturalist and geologist. A road runs round the coast, a total of 56 miles, and passes most points of interest, and a minor road, known as The String and originally built by Telford in 1817, cuts across the island from Brodick to Blackwaterfoot. Just north of Brodick are the Isle of Arran Heritage Museum (1000-1300, 1400-1700 Mon.-Fri., May-Sep.; £1, child 50p), housed in an 18thC croft, and Brodick Castle and Gardens (castle 1300-1700 May-Sep.; gardens 0930-sunset all year; £2.40, child £1.20), the seat of the dukes of Hamilton. It dates in part from the 15thC, with 17thC and 19thC additions, and contains a fine collection of silver, porcelain and paintings, including works by Turner and Watteau. Lochranza, at the north end of the island, has the ferry to Claonaig in Kintyre, and is said to be the place where Robert the Bruce (see **A-Z**) first landed on his return from exile on Rathlin Island. Nearby is the picturesque ruin of 13th-14thC Lochranza Castle. Halfway down the west coast is Machrie Moor, which is rich in prehistoric remains – there are six stone circles and several burial chambers within a few miles of each other. From Blackwaterfoot you can walk 2 miles north along the coast to King's Cave, one of the numerous caves which claim to be the site of Robert the Bruce's encounter with the spider. The walls are decorated with carvings of hunting scenes. Off Lamlash on the east coast is Holy Island, an impressive, steep-sided island rising to 1030 ft. It is a nature reserve, reached by boat from Lamlash. On its west side is a cave that was used as a retreat by 7thC St. Molaise, and there are early Christian and Viking carvings on the walls.

Ayr: Pop: 50,000. Tourist Information (all year), 39 Sandgate, tel: 0292-284196. The town of Ayr straddles the river of the same name, and its extensive beach stretching round the bay has long ensured its position as a popular seaside resort. It is also intimately associated with Robert Burns (see **A-Z**), who lived nearby. A busy town, Ayr is nonetheless attractive, with golf courses, Scotland's premier racecourse, a fine theatre and good shopping, and it makes an excellent base for exploring Burns Country. The Tam o'Shanter Inn on the High

St, where the escapade described in Burns' famous poem is believed to have begun, is now a museum (0930-1700; 35p, child 25p). Also worth a look is the Auld Kirk, built in 1655, where Burns was baptized. See **EXCURSION 1**.

Balmoral: In 1845 Queen Victoria and Prince Albert first visited Balmoral, and in 1852 Prince Albert paid £31,000 for the castle and estate. With meticulous attention to detail he remodelled the royal retreat, personally supervising its decoration and even designing a Balmoral tartan. It became a favourite haunt of Queen Victoria, who fell in love with the Scottish Highlands, and Britain's royal family still takes a holiday here each summer. See **EXCURSION 10**.

Banks: See **Money**.

Ben Nevis: At 4406 ft, Ben Nevis is the highest mountain in the British Isles. It lies about 5 miles southeast of Fort William, from where it appears as a great, rounded hump. In order to get a good view of its dramatic north face, you must go to Banavie (see **EXCURSION 2**), at the start of the Caledonian Canal. A well-maintained footpath leads from Achintee Farm in Glen Nevis (car park) to the summit, and the round trip takes about 6 hr for a fit adult. The climb should only be attempted by experienced walkers with proper hill-walking equipment; snow can remain on the summit all year round. See **EXCURSION 2**, **Walking**.

Best Buys: Traditional Scottish products that make good souvenirs include Harris Tweed, hand-woven in the Outer Hebrides (see **Hebrides**), a hard-wearing woollen cloth coloured with natural dyes. You can buy the material by the yard, or made up into suits, jackets, hats and skirts. Scotland is famous for its top-quality woollen clothing, especially the distinctive designs of Shetland and Fair Isle, and the quality knitwear of the Borders. And of course there is the tartan. This plaid pattern comes in many colour combinations, each traditionally associated with one of Scotland's clans. You can buy rugs, scarves,

skirts, jackets, trousers and kilts in your own clan tartan. Shops which specialize in tartan will find out which clan your surname is affiliated to (if it is of Scottish descent). There are many craft shops throughout the country selling hand-crafted items made from traditionally Scottish materials such as silver, glass, pottery, driftwood, whalebone and stone. Edinburgh Crystal and Caithness Glass produce top-quality glassware. Silver jewellery from Orkney is especially attractive, with pieces often inspired by ancient designs unearthed from local archaeological sites. You can take home a taste of Scotland in a tin of traditional shortbread (a rich butter biscuit), Dundee marmalade, heather honey or Scottish sweets, such as Edinburgh Rock. You will find a vast selection of single-malt whiskies (see **Drinks**), and there are whisky-based liqueurs like Drambuie, and warming ginger wine, made by Crabbie's of Leith. Other foodstuffs, such as smoked salmon and haggis (see **Food**), can be delivered all over the world by mail order; ask at the shop.

Bicycle & Motorcycle Hire: Bicycles can be rented from locations all over Scotland; the local Tourist Information office will direct you to the nearest hire firm. Prices range from around £5 per day for a 3-speed runabout to £10 per day for a 15-speed mountain bike. A returnable cash deposit of around £20 is usually asked for. Mopeds and motorcycles are not available for hire.

Blair Atholl: See EXCURSION 11.

Boat Trips: A number of companies, including Caledonian Macbrayne (see **Ferries**), offer one- to three-day cruises among the islands of Scotland's west coast. These vary from a day trip in a converted fishing boat to watch seals and seabirds, costing around £5, to a multi-day cruise aboard the luxurious *Hebridean Princess*, where a ticket can cost £300-2000. One of the most popular cruises is a day trip from Oban to the beautiful and famous island of Iona (see **EXCURSION 5**). You can also take a boat trip on one of the country's larger inland lochs, in particular Loch Ness and Loch Lomond (see **EXCURSION 2**), and on Loch Awe (see **EXCURSION 4**), sometimes on beautifully restored steamboats. For details, contact the local Tourist Information office. For further information on *Hebridean Princess* cruises, contact Hebridean Island Cruises Ltd, FREEPOST, Bank Newton, Skipton, North Yorkshire, BD23 1BR.

Bonnie Prince Charlie (1720-88): Prince Charles Edward Stuart was the charismatic leader of the Jacobite rebellion of 1745, which attempted to replace a Stuart king on the throne, following the deposition of his grandfather, James VII and II, in 1689, and the subsequent Treaty of Union in 1707, which joined Scotland and England to form the United Kingdom. His doomed campaign to regain the throne is the subject of many romantic tales and famous folk songs, such as *Will Ye No' Come Back Again* and the *Skye Boat Song*. Born in exile in France, the Young Pretender (as he was also known) arrived in Scotland for the first time in July 1745, and raised his standard at Glenfinnan (see **EXCURSION 5**), gathering about him an army of Highlanders opposed to the Union and to the Hanoverian monarch, George II. They marched south, successfully at first, taking Perth and setting up court at the Palace of Holyroodhouse (see **EDINBURGH-ATTRACTIONS**), before defeating Government forces at the Battle of Prestonpans. His campaign reached as far south as Derby, only 130 miles from London, but his army was small and his resources limited, and support for his cause was much less than he had anticipated. He retreated into Scotland and was finally routed on 16 April 1746, at the bloody massacre of Culloden (see **EXCURSION 8**). The prince escaped into the mountains and spent several months in hiding while Government soldiers tried to hunt him down. Despite a price of £30,000 on his head, not one Highlander betrayed him. He kept on the move, living rough in caves, aided by friendly clans, and had several close shaves. The most famous was his escape from South Uist to Skye, under the very noses of the Redcoats, disguised as the maidservant of Flora Macdonald, the daughter of one of his influential supporters. He finally took ship back to France on 20 Sep. 1746, never to return.

Brochs: A broch is a circular dry-stone tower, often with hollow walls, that is thought to have served as a fortified home for some of Scotland's early inhabitants. There are the remains of around 500 brochs in Scotland, mostly situated near the coast in the northern part of the country and in the islands. The best preserved are on Mousa (see **EXCURSION 9**), in Orkney and near Glenelg on the mainland (see **EXCURSION 6**).

Burns, Robert (1759-96): The poet Robert Burns is known and loved the world over through such classics as *Tam o'Shanter*, *My Love is like a Red, Red Rose* and *Auld Lang Syne*. He was born on a small farm in Alloway (see **EXCURSION 1**), its 7.5 acres having to support a family of seven children. Although they were poor, Burns' parents ensured their children were well educated, and while still in his teens the young Robert was already beginning to write. But a love affair with a local girl, Jean Armour, almost forced him to leave his homeland. Threatened with prosecution by her father, he planned to emigrate to Jamaica, and to raise the price of the voyage he had a collection of his poems published in Kilmarnock. Such was the success of the now famous Kilmarnock Edition, that he decided to go to Edinburgh instead, where a second edition was published. It is from these Edinburgh days, when he was a member of a drinking club called the Crochallan Fencibles, and was involved in a secret love affair with a Mrs Agnes MacLehose (the 'Clarinda' of his poems), that his somewhat distorted image as a hard-drinking womanizer derives. Despite this brief relationship, he returned to Ayrshire to marry Jean Armour and together they raised a family. While living at Ellisland Farm near Dumfries (see **EXCURSION 1**), Burns completed two of his most famous works: *Tam* *o'Shanter*, a tale of witchcraft set around the Alloway of his youth, and *Auld Lang Syne*. He died at the age of 37, but left behind him a copious body of work, ranging from songs and poetry to hundreds of letters. His birthday, 25 Jan., is marked all over the world by Burns Suppers, a special dinner at which his poetry is recited, and a meal of haggis (see **Food**) is washed down with whisky.

Buses: Scottish Citylink runs frequent coach services connecting Glasgow and Edinburgh to destinations all over Scotland at very reasonable prices. For example, Edinburgh to Ullapool (7 hr 10 min) costs only £18 return. Tickets should be bought in advance at bus stations or through a travel agent, and reservations are recommended during summer. For details of timetables and fares, call at St. Andrew's Bus Station, Edinburgh, tel: 031-5575717, or Buchanan Bus Station, Glasgow, tel: 041-3329191. A Travelpass card (see **Transport**) is valid on selected Citylink routes. Local bus companies run services connecting the main towns to outlying areas. For details of these buses, contact the local Tourist Information office.

Callander: See EXCURSION 3.

Cameras & Photography: The Scottish landscape is a constant source of inspiration to the keen photographer, and you will probably use more film than you had planned. Stock up in cities, because film will usually be more expensive in small country shops. Most major brands of film are sold in chemists, newsagents, department stores and souvenir shops, as well as specialist camera shops. There are many shops throughout the country that offer same-day processing. Note that there are restrictions on photography in certain museums and art galleries, so check at the reception desk before snapping away.

Aberdeen

Camping & Caravanning: This is a popular form of accommodation for summer visitors to Scotland, and there is a large number of
excellent sites to choose from. The Scottish Tourist Board (see **Tourist
Information**) issues an annual guidebook, *Scotland: Camping &
Caravan Parks*, which lists details and prices of over 400 parks throughout the country (available from bookshops and the STB, £3.25). Prices
range from £2.50-6 per caravan/tent per night, depending on facilities.
Note that caravans are not permitted to park overnight in car parks or
lay-bys. For backpackers and hill walkers, wild camping is possible in
the more remote areas of the country. Wild camping is free, and no official permits are required, but always try to obtain permission from the
landowner first, and never leave any litter behind.

Car Hire: Cars can be rented in most large towns. You must be over
21 and in possession of a full driving licence with at least 12 months'
experience. A large cash deposit will be required unless you are paying
by credit card. Prices and systems of charging vary considerably among
rental companies, so make sure you are aware of the full cost, including insurance, VAT, mileage and any other surcharges. Small, local
firms often charge much lower prices than the nationwide chains; it
may be worth telephoning round and comparing quotes, especially for
short-term, low-mileage hire. Rates can range from £10 per day plus 6p
per mile, to £100 per week unlimited mileage for a small car (e.g. Ford
Fiesta) and £200 per week unlimited mileage for a family saloon (e.g.
Vauxhall Cavalier).
Edinburgh: Avis, 100 Dalry Rd, tel: 031-3376363; Arnold Clark,
Lochrin Pl., tel: 031-2284747; Hertz, 10 Picardy Pl., tel: 031-5568311.
Glasgow: Avis, 161 North St, tel: 041-2212827; Arnold Clark, St.
George's Rd, tel: 041-2219517; Hertz, 106 Waterloo St, tel: 041-
2487736.

Carnegie, Andrew (1835-1919): The famous industrialist and
philanthropist Andrew Carnegie was born in a humble weaver's cottage
in Dunfermline (see **EXCURSION 12**). He emigrated to America where he
built a vast industrial empire based on iron and steel, and went on to
become one of the richest men in the world. Having made his fortune,

he spent his latter years giving away millions of dollars to worthy causes in Britain and America, believing that 'the man who dies rich, dies disgraced'.

Climate: Scotland has a reputation for wet and miserable weather, but this is not surprising when you consider that most visitors come in July and Aug., which are the two wettest months of the year! By far the best time to visit Scotland is in the spring, between mid-April and the end of June. Average temperatures are only 7-13°C, but rainfall is at its lowest, there are many sunny days, and in the north in June it is dark for only 4-5 hr out of 24. The scenery is at its best too, with rhododendrons and bluebells in bloom, and snow patches lingering on the higher mountains. July and Aug. are slightly warmer (average temperature 14-15°C) but much wetter, and the midges (small biting flies) are at their worst. Note that the north and west of the country are noticeably wetter than the south and east. Autumn (Sep. & Oct.) is another good time to visit, when it is often dry and sunny and the hills are purple with heather. Winter (Nov.-Mar.) sees snow and rain and long, dark nights, but is popular with skiers, climbers and hill walkers, and of course there is the traditional Scottish Hogmanay (New Year's Eve) to celebrate.

Coll & Tiree: Pop: 1000. Tourist Information, Argyll Sq., Oban, tel: 0631-63122. These islands lie about 8 miles northwest of Mull (see **EXCURSION 5**) and can be reached by ferry from Oban (see **Ferries**) or by the daily Loganair flight from Glasgow to Tiree (see **Airports**). These islands enjoy what must be the most favourable climate in Scotland, an annual rainfall of less than 50 in and more hours of sunshine than anywhere else in the country (Tiree's weather station records an average of over 220 hr of sunshine for May). The main drawback is the constant wind, from which there is no shelter, but the heavy Atlantic swell has made the islands' west coast the 'Hawaii of the North', and draws surfers and boardsailors from all over Britain. Both islands are relatively flat, but while Tiree is green and fertile, Coll is mostly moorland. The islanders survive on a combination of farming, lobster-fishing and tourism. In addition to walking, bird-watching and angling, visitors can explore the ruins of a 1stC AD fort at Dun Mor Vaul and the 15thC Breachachadh Castle (visits by appointment, tel: 083793-444) on Tiree, restored and used as a family home by Maj. Maclean-Bristol. From Ben Hynish (462 ft) at the southwest end of Tiree you can look across 10 miles of sea to the famous Skerryvore Lighthouse, built 1838-43 by Alan Stevenson (an uncle of Robert Louis Stevenson – see **A-Z**), which stands on a rock only 10 ft above mean sea level.

Colonsay & Oronsay: Pop: 130. Tourist Information, Argyll Sq., Oban, tel: 0631-63122. These islands, linked by a sand spit at low water, can be reached by car ferry from Oban, or from Kennacraig near Tarbert (see **EXCURSION 4, Ferries**). They offer good walking and bird-watching, and there is a hotel, some holiday cottages and a few B&Bs. Kiloran Gardens (all reasonable times; free), on Colonsay, are famous for the displays of rhododendrons (at their colourful best in May and June), azaleas, acacias and magnolias. On Colonsay's much smaller neighbour Oronsay (named after Oran, St. Columba's – see **A-Z** – companion) you will find the remains of a 14thC Augustinian priory, built on the site of the original church founded by Columba in the 6thC.

Complaints: If you have been overcharged or have any other complaint about a hotel, restaurant or other establishment, ask to see the owner or manager of the premises. If he or she is unable to settle the matter to your satisfaction, you can report the matter to the Scottish Tourist Board (see **Tourist Information**) or to the consumer advice department of the local regional council (look in the telephone directory under Trading Standards).

Consulates: Embassies are located in London.
Australia – Australian Consulate, Hobart House, 80 Hanover St, Edinburgh, tel: 031-2266271.
USA – American Consulate General, 3 Regent Terr., Edinburgh, tel: 031-5568315.

Edinburgh from the Castle

O HEAR US WHEN WE CRY

TO THEE

FOR THOSE IN PERIL ON

THE SEA

Covenanters: During the reign of Charles I (1625-49), the king tried to standardize the form of church service throughout England and Scotland, forcing the introduction of bishops and the *Anglican Prayer Book* into the Scottish Church. This resulted in rebellion by the staunch adherents of the Presbyterian Reformation, who signed a National Covenant at Edinburgh in 1638. This document pledged allegiance to the principles of the Reformation (see **A-Z**): simplicity of the church service, equality of all ministers (i.e. no bishops) and the separation of the Church from the State. The Covenanters, as they came to be known, were cruelly oppressed by Government forces for several decades, culminating in the reign of James VII and II (1685-88), when the penalty for worshipping as a Covenanter was death. They were forced to meet in secret and often held services outdoors in hidden hollows in the hills. Their ordeal ended with the accession of the Protestant William of Orange in 1688 and the abolition of bishops.

Credit Cards: See **Money**.

Crime & Theft: Although crimes against visitors to Scotland are relatively rare, it is sensible to take the usual precautions against theft. Leave any valuables in the hotel safe and not in your room. Beware of pickpockets in crowded areas such as shopping centres and city railway stations. Always lock your car and keep any items of value locked out of sight in the boot. Report any theft to the police immediately, and if your passport has been lost or stolen, contact your consulate also. See **Consulates**, **Emergency Numbers**, **Insurance**, **Police**.

Culloden, Battle of: See EXCURSION 8, **Bonnie Prince Charlie**.

Currency: The British unit of currency is the pound sterling (£), equal to 100 pence (p). Banknotes come in denominations of £50 (red), £20 (purple), £10 (brown), £5 (blue) and £1 (green). The coins are £1, 50p, 20p, 10p, 5p, 2p and 1p. Note that the three Scottish banks – Bank of Scotland, Royal Bank of Scotland and Clydesdale Bank – all issue their own distinctive banknotes which are different in appearance (but not in value) from their English equivalents. English £1 notes are no longer in circulation. Scottish banknotes are occasionally refused in shops in England (although, except for the £1 note, they are legal tender), so it is advisable to exchange them for English notes before heading south of the border. See **Money**.

Customs: Visitors to the far northwest of Scotland, and especially to Skye, Lewis, Harris and North Uist (see **Hebrides**), should be aware that there is a strong tradition of Sabbath observance in this area. This means that everything closes down on Sun., including shops, pubs, ferries and public transport, and this should be allowed for when planning your trip.

Disabled People: Advice for disabled visitors can be obtained from the Scottish Tourist Board (see **Tourist Information**), which also publishes a booklet, *Holidays with Care*. In addition, the National Trust for Scotland (see **A-Z**) supplies a free booklet detailing the castles, gardens and other properties under its care that have facilities for the disabled.

Drinks: Scotland is world-famous for its whisky (the name comes from the Gaelic *uisge beatha*, meaning 'water of life'). There are over 2000 brands of whisky to choose from. Over 100 of these are single malts, distilled purely from malted barley and aged in wooden casks, each as distinctive to the experienced palate as a classic wine. The rest are blends, mixtures of 15 to 50 grain whiskies (distilled from a mix of malted barley with other, unmalted cereals), with a smaller amount of malt whiskies. A popular after-dinner drink is a whisky liqueur such as Drambuie, sweetened with honey, or Columba Cream, a smooth blend of whisky and cream.

Scotland's breweries produce some excellent beers. Names to look out for include draught Belhaven, Maclay's, Caledonian, Greenmantle and McEwan's 80/-. Beers are often classified in the traditional manner, as 60/-, 70/- or 80/- in order of increasing strength. These are roughly equivalent to English mild, bitter and best. Distinctive bottled beers include the organic Golden Promise from Caledonian, and Traquair Ale, brewed in the Earl of Traquair's private 18thC brew house.

The country's most popular non-alcoholic drink is, of course, tea,

available along with coffee and soft drinks in countless tearooms and cafés all over Scotland. Mineral water is becoming increasingly popular, and in addition to the usual French brands there are some Scottish mineral waters, such as Highland Spring and Strathmore.

Driving: You will need your driving licence (foreign licences can be used in the UK for up to 12 months) and also registration and insurance documents if you are bringing your own vehicle. Driving is on the left-hand side of the road. The wearing of seat belts is compulsory for the driver and front-seat passenger, and also for back-seat passengers where seat belts are fitted. Road regulations are detailed in the booklet *The Highway Code*, available from the AA, RAC and many bookshops. Most road signs conform to international standards. Speed limits are 30 or 40 mph/48 or 64 kph in built-up areas, 60 mph/96 kph on single-carriageway main roads and 70 mph/112 kph on dual carriageways and motorways. Driving conditions are generally good.

Driving in the city centre in Glasgow and Edinburgh can be frustrating because of congestion, especially during the peak hours 0800-0900 and 1700-1800. In addition, Glasgow has a rather confusing one-way system. In the more remote areas of Scotland you will often come across single-track roads with passing places. These are wide enough for only one vehicle at a time, so you must drive carefully and use the passing places, usually marked with a striped pole, to allow oncoming traffic to pass. These passing places should also be used to allow following traffic to overtake you – local people are often frustrated by tourists who drive slowly but refuse to allow them to pass. Never park in a passing place; use only official lay-bys and car parks. Many roads in the Highlands and Islands are unfenced, so be on the lookout for sheep, cattle and deer that have strayed onto the road. See **Accidents & Breakdowns**, **Car Hire**, **Insurance**, **Parking**, **Petrol**.

Dumfries: Pop: 32,400. Tourist Information (all year), Whitesands, tel: 0387-53862. The town straddles the River Nith and its most attractive face can be seen along the waterfront. It was here at Greyfriars Friary (opposite the present Greyfriars Church on Castle St) that Robert the Bruce (see **A-Z**) murdered the Red Comyn. Robert Burns (see **A-Z**) lived for many years in the town too. At Burns House (1000-1300, 1400-1700 Mon.-Sat.) on Burns St, you can see where the poet spent the last three years of his life, together with a museum and memorabilia. Burns drank in the Globe Inn near the High St and it still serves a good ale. The Robert Burns Centre (1000-2000 Mon.-Sat., 1400-1700 Sun., April-Sep.; 1000-1300, 1400-1700 Tue.-Sat., Oct.-Mar.; exhibition free, audio-visual presentation 50p) on Mill Rd carries an audio-visual presentation of the poet's life, while at St. Michael's Church you can see the Burns family pew and in the churchyard the mausoleum where his body lies. Dumfries Museum (1000-1300, 1400-1700 Mon.-Sat., 1400-1700 Sun.; free, camera obscura 75p, child 25p), in an 18thC windmill tower on Corbelly Hill, details the local history. Atop the tower is a camera obscura. On the A 76 6 miles north of Dumfries is Ellisland Farm (tel: 0387-74426 to view; free), where Burns unsuccessfully experimented with new farming techniques and successfully wrote *Tam o'Shanter* and *Auld Lang Syne*. See **EXCURSION 1**.

Dundee: Pop: 182,000. Tourist Information (all year), 4 City Sq., tel: 0382-27723. Dundee, set on the north bank of the River Tay, was once famous as a shipbuilding centre, and as the city of 'jute, jam and journalism', after three of its principal products (jute is a natural fibre used to make sacks and rope). Today it is a busy commercial and industrial city, largely dependent on the North Sea oil business. Modern developments have left little of historical interest, but there are one or two places worth visiting, such as the McManus Galleries (1000-1700; free), the city's main museum, on Albert Sq., and the RRS *Discovery* (1400-1700 April, May & Sep., 1000-1700 June-Aug.; £1.75, child £1), the Dundee-built ship that carried Capt. Scott's ill-fated expedition to the Antarctic, which is on display at the waterfront. See **EXCURSION 12**.

Dunfermline: Pop: 52,000. Tourist Information (Easter-Sep.), Abbot House, Maygate, tel: 0383-720999. Originally belonging to the Church but later given royal burgh status which afforded it special trading privileges, the town can boast both an abbey and a palace. Dunfermline Abbey (0930-1200, 1300-1700; £1, child 50p) on Monastery St, was built by Queen Margaret, wife of Malcolm III (1057-93), and later became a Benedictine abbey. Robert the Bruce (see **A-Z**), who died of leprosy in 1327, is buried in the choir. The Palace lies just below the abbey. The story of Andrew Carnegie (see **A-Z**) is told at the Andrew Carnegie Birthplace Museum (1100-1700 Mon.-Sat., 1400-1700 Sun.; free) on Moodie St. See **EXCURSION 12**.

Dunkeld: See **EXCURSION 11**.

Eating Out: The restaurant scene in Scotland has improved greatly over the last ten years or so, and there has been a surge of renewed pride in the use of fresh, imaginatively prepared, local produce. The towns and cities offer a wide range of eating establishments, from top-class French restaurants, through the whole spectrum of national cuisines (though Chinese, Indian and Italian are by far the most common), to traditional fish-and-chip shops, cafés and fast-food outlets. But it is in the rural areas that the best Scottish restaurants are to be found. Not only is there good local food to be enjoyed, but the setting of some

of the restaurants is exceptional – country houses, castles, old cottages and converted barns and farmhouses. Many of these restaurants also boast excellent wine lists. Prices for meals can vary from under £5 to more than £20 per head (exc. drinks). Good-value lunches can be enjoyed in country pubs and hotel bars, usually from 1200-1500, while dinner is generally served from 1800-2200. The Scottish Tourist Board (see **Tourist Information**) supports a scheme called The Taste of Scotland, which encourages the imaginative use of Scottish produce, and publishes an annual guide (£2.50) to over 350 of Scotland's best restaurants, available from bookshops and Tourist Information offices. In the **RESTAURANTS** topic sections in this guidebook, Inexpensive refers to a meal for one, exc. drinks, costing under £10, Moderate £10-20 and Expensive over £20. See **EDINBURGH-RESTAURANTS**, **GLASGOW-RESTAURANTS**, **Drinks**, **Food**.

Edinburgh: Pop: 439,000. Tourist Information (all year), Waverley Market, Princes St, tel: 031-5522727. Scotland's capital, set among rocky hills on the southern shores of the Firth of Forth, is unrivalled in Britain for the beauty of its setting. Rich in historical, architectural and cultural attractions, it is at the top of the list of most first-time visitors to the country.

The oldest surviving building in Edinburgh is St. Margaret's Chapel, on the highest point of the Castle Rock, dating from the 11thC, though there has been some form of defence here since the 6thC. The chapel was built after the Scottish capital was moved to Edinburgh from Dunfermline (see **EXCURSION 12**, **A-Z**), and was surrounded by early fortifications and a small village that grew up close to the safety of the castle walls. Over the centuries this village spread down the Royal Mile, the road that led from the Castle to the 12thC Abbey of Holyrood, and later to the 15thC Palace of Holyroodhouse, seat of Scotland's kings and queens until the Union of the Crowns in 1603. This straggling town of towering tenements, hemmed in by a 16thC city wall, was known as the Old Town. Squalor and overcrowding led the city fathers in the 18thC to begin extending the city to the north. The result was the classical elegance of the New Town, one of the world's best surviving examples of late 18th/early 19thC urban planning. The city continued to expand throughout the 19th and 20thC, swallowing a number of villages, including Dean Village, Duddingston and Cramond, which have nevertheless maintained their distinct identities to the present day. Since 1947, Edinburgh has achieved international fame through its festival, an annual arts extravaganza which takes place in the last three weeks of Aug., accompanied by numerous other attractions like the Festival Fringe, the Jazz, Film and Book festivals, and the Military Tattoo. Visitors can also enjoy the city's excellent museums and art galleries, its diverse restaurants and pubs, and shopping with a view on world-famous Princes St. In addition, there are many lovely walks among the city's hills and parks. Edinburgh's rich architectural heritage and magnificent natural setting prompted Robert Louis Stevenson (see **A-Z**) to describe it as 'this profusion of eccentricities, this dream in masonry and living rock'. It is a city you will enjoy exploring. See **EDINBURGH, EXCURSION 13**.

Edinburgh Tattoo
Edinburgh Festival

Electricity: Standard voltage is 240 V/50 Hz AC. Adaptors will be required for all foreign appliances and transformers too for American appliances. Shaver sockets are international standard, two-pin design, 240 V.

Emergency Numbers:

Police	999
Ambulance	999
Fire brigade	999
Mountain rescue	999
Coastguard	999

Braemar Highland Gathering

Events:

1 January: Ba' Game (massive game of street football), Kirkwall, Orkney; *Late January:* Up Helly Aa (Viking festival), Lerwick, Shetland.

March: International Folk Music Festival, Edinburgh.

April: International Science Festival, Edinburgh; Festival of Traditional Music, Tobermory, Isle of Mull; Shetland Folk Festival; Jazz Festival, Isle of Bute.

May: International Gathering of the Clans, Inverness; Mayfest (cultural festival), Glasgow.

June: Burns Festival, Ayrshire; International Jazz Festival, Glasgow; Lanimer Day (historic festival, with a parade, games, etc.), Lanark; Royal Highland Show (Scotland's main agricultural show), Edinburgh.

July–September: Highland Games, various locations.

July: International Highland Games, Aviemore.

August: Folk Music Festival, Isle of Skye; Military Tattoo, International Festival, Festival Fringe, Film Festival, Jazz Festival, Edinburgh; Glenfinnan Gathering and Highland Games; Cowal Highland Gathering, Dunoon; World Pipe Band Championships, Glasgow.

September: Braemar Highland Gathering; Ben Nevis Race (fell runners compete on the UK's highest mountain), Fort William; Glasgow Marathon.

October: National Mod (Gaelic music festival), at a different venue each year.

30 November: St. Andrew's Day Celebrations, St. Andrews.

31 December: Fireball Ceremony, Stonehaven.

Full details of annual events in Scotland can be obtained from the Scottish Tourist Board's free booklet *Events in Scotland* (see **Tourist Information**). See **What's On**.

Ferries: There are numerous ferries serving Scotland's many islands. The great majority of these are run by two large companies: Caledonian Macbrayne serves the Firth of Clyde and the Western Isles, while P&O Scottish Ferries serves Orkney and Shetland. Services are frequent in summer (May-Sep.), less so in winter. Note that some ferries in the Western Isles do not operate on Sun. (see **Customs**). If you plan to take your car to the islands during the high season (July and Aug.), you are recommended to make advance reservations, either through a travel agent or direct with the ferry companies (see telephone numbers below). For those intending to use a number of Caledonian Macbrayne ferry services, there are special Island Hopscotch tickets (£88.50 for eight days, £132 for 15 days) which work out cheaper than buying individual tickets for each ferry. More information is available from main Tourist Information offices or from the ferry companies themselves: Caledonian Macbrayne, The Ferry Terminal, Gourock PA19 1QP, tel: 0475-33755; P&O Scottish Ferries, PO Box 5, Jameson's Quay, Aberdeen AB9 8DL, tel: 0224-572615. See **Boat Trips**.

Food: Scotland is world-famous for its top-quality meats: prime beef from the Aberdeen Angus herds, tender lamb, and mouthwatering venison from the red deer that roam the hills. And then there are grouse from the moors, salmon and trout from the lochs and rivers, and of course the rich harvest of the sea: juicy lobster, prawns, crab, oysters, scallops, mussels, herring, haddock and cod. Traditional soups include Cock-a-leekie (made with chicken, onion and leek), Partan Bree (a creamy crab soup) and Cullen Skink (a filling broth of smoked haddock, milk, onion and potato). Loch Fyne kippers (smoked herring) are a popular breakfast dish, or you could try an Arbroath Smokie (haddock smoked over birch or oak twigs) or Finnan Haddie (haddock smoked over peat). Scottish salmon is famed worldwide for its quality and flavour, and is equally delicious poached, baked or smoked.

A main course of beef, lamb or venison might be followed by a dessert based on Scottish fruit (e.g. raspberries, gooseberries or rhubarb), or a dish of Athol Brose, a rich blend of cream, whisky and oatmeal. Oatmeal turns up in many Scottish dishes: as porridge, taken at breakfast with milk and salt (no true Scot puts sugar on his porridge!); in oatcakes, delicious with cheese and fruit after dinner; as a coating on fried herring; and in what must be the best known of Scottish dishes – haggis. This famous pudding is prepared using the minced liver, heart and lungs of a sheep, mixed with oatmeal, onion, suet and seasoning. The mixture is used to stuff the stomach bag of a sheep, and the whole is cooked in boiling water. It tastes much better than it sounds! Haggis is served with 'bashed neeps and chappit tatties' (mashed turnip and potato) and is traditionally eaten on Burns Night (25 Jan.). See **Eating Out**.

Forth Road & Rail Bridges: This pair of spectacular bridges span the Firth of Forth at Queensferry, about 8 miles west of Edinburgh. A ferry plied across the water here for at least 900 years, since the days when Queen Margaret, wife of Malcolm III (1057-93), travelled regularly between Edinburgh and her palace in Dunfermline (see **A-Z**). In 1890 the Forth rail bridge was built at a cost of £3.2 million. At the time it was the largest bridge in the world – 54,000 tons of steel were used in its construction – and painting its 45 acre surface is a never-ending task. The neighbouring Forth road bridge, which stretches 1.4 miles across the firth from South to North Queensferry, was opened in 1964 at a cost of £19.5 million. Its 512 ft towers support two steel cables, each 6 ft thick, from which a four-lane highway and a cycle/footpath are suspended. See **EXCURSION 12**.

Fort William: Pop: 4200. Tourist Information (all year), Cameron Sq., tel: 0397-3781. The principal town of the western Highlands, and a centre for road and rail transport, Fort William is situated beneath Ben Nevis (see **A-Z**), at the southern end of the Caledonian Canal. It is a major tourist centre with a wide range of facilities. In Cameron Sq. is the West Highland Museum (1000-1300, 1400-1700 Mon.-Sat., June-Sep., 0930-1730 July & Aug.; 50p, child 20p). It has an interesting collection of historical material, information on natural history, displays on

aluminium smelting (a local industry), the Caledonian Canal and unusual ascents of Ben Nevis. At the south end of the High St is the Scottish Crafts and Ben Nevis Exhibition, which consists mainly of a large souvenir and crafts shop. At the pier nearby you will find the Crannog Seafood Restaurant, tel: 0397-5589, an excellent place to sample the local seafood. The vessel *Souter's Lass* offers 1.5 hr cruises from the pier down Loch Linnhe to seal-haunted islands (1000, 1200, 1400 & 1600, plus 1945 weekdays only; £4, child £2). The Lochaber Leisure Centre (1000-2100 Mon.-Fri., 1000-1700 Sat. & Sun.; £1, child 50p), Belford Rd, tel: 0397-4359, has a swimming pool, and also offers a sauna and solarium, squash, tennis, crazy golf and a fitness room. Parascending is available at the Town Pier, £17 per person, tel: 08552-502. For railway enthusiasts, ScotRail runs a special train drawn by a historic steam locomotive between Fort William and Mallaig (dep. Fort William daily June-Sep.). Further information can be obtained from Fort William Transport Centre, tel: 0397-3791. About 4 miles north of the town on the A 82 is a right turn to the Aonach Mor Gondola, tel: 0397-5825. This winter ski centre has a gondola (cable car) that stays open all summer. Ride from the car park and café to the Snowgoose Restaurant at 2300 ft (0930-evening; return £3.70, child £2.50, family £10). There is an exhibition and shop, mountain walks, ranger service and mountain bike hire. See **EXCURSION 2**.

Glasgow: Pop: 695,000. Tourist Information (all year), 35 St. Vincent Pl., tel: 041-2044400. Glasgow is Scotland's largest city, and one of its newest tourist attractions. Over the past 15 years there has been a concerted effort to improve the city's image and dispel its largely unwarranted reputation as a violent, hard-drinking city, cursed by slums, unemployment and industrial decline. The campaign has been highly successful, and while many social problems remain, Glasgow's appearance and appeal have improved enormously, with the restoration of many grand, Victorian buildings, the construction of attractive new shopping centres, and the opening of new cultural sites such as the Burrell Collection adding to what has always been a city of great cultural and historic interest.

Glasgow's beginnings can be traced back to the 8thC, when the Celtic missionary St. Mungo (also known as St. Kentigern) built a church on the bank of the Molendinar Burn, near the River Clyde, at a spot called Glas Ghu, meaning 'green hollow', though often translated as 'dear green place'. Glasgow Cathedral was founded on the site of Mungo's church in the 12thC, and the university was founded in 1451, making the small but growing city a major centre of religion and learning. The 18thC saw the phenomenal growth of trade with the New World, and Glasgow was ideally placed as a port for transatlantic commerce. Sugar and rum, and nearly half of the tobacco coming into the UK, arrived at Glasgow. Fortunes were made – the city's merchants became so rich and powerful that they were called the Tobacco Lords – and lost when the American War of Independence cut off the trade. But in the 19thC, cotton mills, iron smelting, coal mining, shipbuilding and heavy engineering provided new fortunes, and saw Glasgow rise to prominence as the quintessential Victorian city, the Second City of the Empire. Glasgow's ships, steam locomotives and engines were exported all over the world, and the term Clyde-built meant the best there was. But the Depression of the 1930s, and the post-war slump in traditional heavy industries, heralded the city's 20thC decline.

However, the city is now home to the superb art collections of the Kelvingrove Art Gallery, the Hunterian and the Burrell Collection, as well as Scottish Opera and Ballet, the Royal Scottish and BBC Scottish Symphony orchestras, much of the work of Charles Rennie Mackintosh (see **A-Z**), and the varied cultural events of Mayfest – a renaissance rewarded by Glasgow being nominated as the European City of Culture for 1990. See **EXCURSIONS 2 & 3, GLASGOW**.

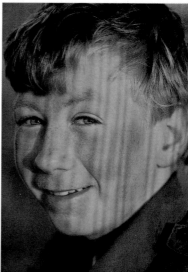

Glencoe Massacre: When William of Orange came to the throne in 1689, he was determined to prove his authority over the unruly Scots, and so demanded that each clan chief should swear an oath of allegiance to him: the deadline for capitulation was set at midnight, 31 Dec. 1691. Macdonald of Glencoe, reluctant to submit, did not take his oath until the last minute, and his papers did not arrive in Edinburgh until a few days after the king's deadline. The Government used this as an excuse to make an example of the troublesome Macdonalds, and ordered Campbell of Glenlyon, an old Macdonald enemy, to carry out the task. The Secretary of State for Scotland, in his written orders, finished: 'I hope the soldiers will not trouble the Government with prisoners.' Campbell and 128 of his soldiers lodged with the Macdonalds (who knew nothing of their guests' true intent and made them welcome) for two weeks and won their confidence. Then, in the early hours of 13 Feb. 1692, the Campbells turned on their hosts, carrying

out the Government's orders to put all Macdonalds under 70 to the sword. Forty clan members were slain, including the chief and his wife; women, children and invalids were not spared. Others perished in the snow-bound hills in their attempts to escape. The site of one of the most evil deeds in Scottish history is commemorated by a plaque near the Clachaig Hotel (see **EXCURSION 2**).

Gleneagles: See **EXCURSION 11**.

Great Glen: This 60 mile-long valley runs in a straight line from Fort William (see **A-Z**) to Inverness (see **A-Z**), its course determined by a major geological fault line. The lochs that lie along the glen are connected by the Caledonian Canal, which permits the passage of small vessels between the Moray Firth and Loch Linnhe. See **EXCURSION 2**.

Gretna Green: See EXCURSION 1.

Guides: Guided coach tours and walking tours are available for all popular tourist areas: ask at Tourist Information offices or travel agents. If you would like to arrange for your own personal guide, contact the Scottish Tourist Guides Association, 25 Regent Terr., Edinburgh EH7 5BS, tel: 031-5574111.

Hawick: See EXCURSION 13.

Health: Under Britain's National Health Service, overseas visitors are eligible for free emergency treatment at hospital accident and emergency departments. Nevertheless, you are strongly recommended to take out adequate medical insurance before your trip. EC nationals can take advantage of reciprocal health care arrangements by filling out form E111 before their trip. Contact your own health service for details. In a medical emergency, tel: 999 and ask for an ambulance. There are 24 hr accident and emergency departments at hospitals in the main cities of Edinburgh, Glasgow, Dundee and Aberdeen. In the Highlands and Islands, the main hospitals are in Inverness and Fort William, and emergency cases in remote areas are often airlifted to one of these sites by helicopter. For less serious complaints, make an appointment to see a local doctor. Your hotel or the local police station will have a list of available doctors and dentists. If visiting the western Highlands in summer, you are strongly advised to take along an insect repellent to combat the hordes of midges (tiny biting flies), which are the scourge of the west coast. See **Emergency Numbers**, **Insurance**.

Hebrides: This name refers to the islands of Scotland's west coast and is derived from the Norse word *Havbredey*, which means 'Isles on the Edge of the Sea'. The islands are generally divided into two groups: the Outer Hebrides (Lewis and Harris, the Uists, Benbecula and Barra), which form a 130 mile-long chain off northwest Scotland, and the Inner Hebrides (Skye, the Small Isles – see **A-Z**, Coll and Tiree – see **A-Z**, Mull, Islay and Jura – see **A-Z**) which lie closer to the mainland. See EXCURSION 5.

Hebrides

Historic Scotland: Formerly known as Historic Buildings and Monuments, this is a government body which looks after Scotland's ancient monuments on behalf of the nation. Most of the sites under the care of HS have standard opening times (see **A-Z**). Principal sites charge a small admission fee and have knowledgeable caretakers who will explain the significance of the site to you. Smaller sites may be free, unattended and open at all reasonble times. A season ticket valid for one year costs £11 and gives free access to all sites. Details can be obtained from Historic Scotland, 20 Brandon St, Edinburgh EH3 5RA, tel: 031-2443101.

Insurance: Overseas visitors are strongly recommended to take out adequate medical and travel insurance before departing for the UK. Your travel agent will be able to recommend a suitable policy. See **Crime & Theft**, **Driving**, **Health**.

Inverness: Pop: 39,500. Tourist Information (all year), 23 Church St, tel: 0463-234353. Inverness is the largest town in the Highlands and capital of the Highland Region, offering a wide variety of shops and services. From the Tourist Information office, turn right and cross the High St opposite the Town House (built 1880), then head up the alley to its right to find Inverness Museum and Art Gallery (0900-1700 Mon.-Sat.; free) in Castle Wynd. This is an excellent modern museum of local history, archaeology and natural history; upstairs, the art gallery displays contemporary Scottish art. Neighbouring Inverness Castle (closed to the public) on its hill top above the river houses local government offices. Across the River Ness from the castle is the pink stone edifice of St. Andrew's Cathedral, built in 1868. Next to it is the Eden Court Theatre, Bishop's Rd, tel: 0463-221718. Opened in 1976, the theatre stages drama, music and dance of all kinds. The complex also includes a small cinema, restaurant and bar. If you follow the road along the northwest bank of the river, heading upstream, you will find Ness Islands Park, a delightful spot for strolls or picnics, set on wooded islands in the river linked together by footbridges. From here Bught Rd leads away from the river to Tomnahurich Bridge; Tomnahurich Hill to the right is a lovely burial ground with pleasant walks and views over the town. The bridge crosses the Caledonian Canal, with good walks to be had along the towpath. Cross the bridge and go right on General Booth Rd, then right again on Canal Rd to Muirtown Locks. From the quay above the locks the *Scot II* offers cruises on Loch Ness. Cruises depart 1015 (2.5 hr, £4, child £2.50) and 1415 (3.5 hr, inc. Urquhart Castle – see **EXCURSION 2**, £6.50, child £4.50) Sun.-Fri., May-Sep. Bookings can be made at the Tourist Information office, or Scot II Cruises, tel: 0463-232955. The ticket office at the quay opens 30 min before departures. See **EXCURSION 8**.

Iona: See **EXCURSION 5**.

Iona Abbey

Islay & Jura: These large islands, the most southerly of the Hebrides (see **A-Z**), lie off the coast of Argyll. They can be reached by ferry from Kennacraig (see **EXCURSION 4**) on West Loch Tarbert.
Islay. Pop: 4000. Tourist Information (April-Oct.), Bowmore, tel: 049681-254. The island has three main villages: Port Ellen, Port Askaig and Bowmore. The landscape is a mix of farmland and moors, and offers excellent walking and bird-watching. The most famous site on the island is Kidalton churchyard, which contains two of the finest carved-stone, Celtic crosses in the country, dating from around AD 800. It lies in the southeast part of the island, 7 miles northeast of Port Ellen.

Another attraction for visitors are Islay's distilleries, which produce strongly-flavoured, peaty malts such as Laphroaig, and the smoother Bunnahabhainn. Contact the Tourist Information office for details of distillery tours.

Jura. Pop: 200. Jura is very different from its close neighbour. Reached by a 10 min ferry crossing from Port Askaig, it is a wild and mountainous place, given over mainly to deerstalking. The Paps of Jura, rising to 2576 ft, provide rugged hill walking, and at the northern end of the island, in the narrow strait between Jura and Scarba, is the famous Corryvreckan whirlpool. Spring tides rush through this gap at up to 10 knots, and underwater ledges force the swirling water into dangerous rips and overfalls. When the east-going tide meets a westerly gale, the roar of the whirlpool can be heard from the mainland, several miles away.

Jedburgh: See EXCURSION 13.

John o'Groats: See EXCURSION 7.

Kelso: See EXCURSION 13.

Kirkcudbright: See EXCURSION 1.

Knox, John (1505-72): Born near Haddington, East Lothian, this 16thC leader of the Scottish Reformation (see **A-Z**) was largely responsible for the establishment of the Protestant faith in Scotland. Originally a Roman Catholic priest, Knox committed himself to Protestantism in 1545, and was minister of St. Giles' Cathedral (see **EDINBURGH-WALK**) from 1559 until his death. Although he is known principally for introducing the austere doctrines of Calvinism, thus setting the pattern of Scottish religious and social life for the following three centuries, he also bequeathed much valuable historical documentation to future generations.

Laundries: Hotels provide a next-day laundry service, but it is expensive. Much cheaper (around £2.50 per load) are the many coin-operated Launderettes found in most large towns and on some camping and caravan sites. Most of these establishments offer a service wash for a slightly higher price, meaning you can leave your laundry in the morning and pick it up, washed and dried, in the afternoon.

Loch Lomond: See EXCURSION 2.

Loch Ness: See EXCURSION 2.

Lost Property: Lost property is usually handed in to the nearest police station, so check there first. If you have left something behind on public transport, contact the head office of the transport company (see **Buses, Ferries, Railways**).

Macbeth (1040-1057): The real-life Macbeth was not the pathetic villain depicted in Shakespeare's famous drama. True, he did come to the throne by slaying Duncan, but he killed the king in battle. Macbeth believed he had a better claim to the throne than his predecessor. The system of succession in those days was an unusual one, in which the king was chosen from eligible members of a broad 'royal family' on his individual merits, rather than through direct filial descent. The system had the disadvantage that there would always be a group who believed that someone else was better qualified to rule, and few kings died a natural death: seven in a row met a violent end. Having disposed of Duncan, Macbeth ruled Scotland wisely and well for 17 years, and was renowned for being very generous towards the Church. But eventually he, in turn, was slain by Duncan's son, Malcolm Canmore.

Macdonald, James Ramsay (1866-1937): Born in Lossiemouth (see EXCURSION 8), Ramsay Macdonald formed the first Labour government in 1924 but failed to bring about the social revolution that many of the party's supporters expected. In 1929 he again led the party to power but in 1931 he resigned, in the face of opposition from the Independent Labour Party, to form a National government with Conservatives and Liberals. The new National government again went to the country in 1931 and was overwhelmingly voted back into office, only to lead the country through the darkest days of the Depression.

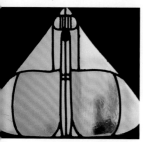

Mackintosh, Charles Rennie (1868-1928): Born in Glasgow, Mackintosh began his professional training in 1884 and became the most celebrated exponent of the 'Glasgow Style', a variation on Art Nouveau, which flourished during the period 1890-1920. Having achieved recognition as an architect through exhibitions in Europe, he went on to design his greatest building, the Glasgow School of Art (see **GLASGOW-WALK**), built 1897-1909 and the first European building in the 'modern style'. Other Mackintosh buildings of note include the Willow Tearooms (see **GLASGOW-WALK**), The Hill House at Helensburgh (see **EXCURSION 2**) and Scotland St School (1904) in Glasgow.

Mary, Queen of Scots (1542-87): Mary was the daughter of James V of Scotland and his French queen, Marie de Guise (Scotland and France were then in alliance against England). She was born in 1542, the same year that her father died, and was proclaimed as Queen of Scots when she was only six days old. A romantic and tragic figure in Scottish history, she claimed the throne of England as well as of Scotland, challenging the legitimacy of her reigning cousin, Elizabeth I. Mary spent most of her childhood in France and arrived in Scotland in 1561, at the age of 18. A Catholic queen in a devoutly Protestant country, she was forced to abdicate after six years, and was imprisoned in the island fortress of Loch Leven. She escaped and tried to return to France, before placing herself at the mercy of Elizabeth. Her cousin, fearful of Mary's claim to her throne, imprisoned the Queen of Scots for the next 20 years, until finally, in 1587, she was beheaded for allegedly plotting to assassinate the monarch.

Money: Foreign currency can be exchanged in banks, at branches of the Thomas Cook travel agency and at exchange bureaux located in the larger cities. Automatic teller machines are common in the larger towns, but check in advance whether your bank card will be accepted by the Scottish banks' machines. Building society teller machines are also widespread. Traveller's cheques are widely accepted throughout Scotland; you will need your passport when cashing them. It is best to exchange cheques and currency in a bank, as they offer much better rates than hotels and exchange bureaux. Major credit cards – Visa, Access, American Express and Diners Club – are widely accepted in hotels, restaurants, shops and ticket offices. See **Crime & Theft**, **Currency**, **Opening Times**.

Mull, Isle of: See EXCURSION 5.

Music: The type of music most commonly associated with Scotland is that of the bagpipes. Pipe music can be heard at many festivals, especially the Edinburgh Military Tattoo and at Highland Games (see **Events**), and there is a museum of piping on the Isle of Skye (see **EXCURSION 5**). Traditional Gaelic music and song can be enjoyed at the annual Mod (see **Events**), while traditional Scots folk songs, performed by local bands, can be heard in many pubs and hotels throughout the country: check out local newspapers and notice boards, or ask at Tourist Information offices.

National Trust for Scotland (NTS): This organization was founded in 1931, with the aim of preserving places of historic interest and natural beauty in Scotland. It is a registered charity supported by members' subscriptions, admission fees and voluntary contributions. It cares for over 100 properties, as different in character as Glencoe (see

EXCURSION 2) and Culzean Castle (see **EXCURSION 1**). Membership costs £15 per year and gives free admission to all NTS properties, and also to a further 300 National Trust properties in the rest of the UK. For further information, contact the NTS head office at 5 Charlotte Sq., Edinburgh EH2 4DU, tel: 031-2265922.

Newspapers: Scotland's national newspapers are the broadsheet *Scotsman* and *Glasgow Herald*, and the tabloid *Daily Record*. UK national dailies are available throughout Scotland, but in the far north and west morning editions do not arrive in the shops until the afternoon. There are numerous local newspapers too, which are good sources of information on local events. See **What's On**.

Nightlife: Outside the larger towns, nightlife is confined to a drink in the local pub, perhaps to the accompaniment of a folk singer on Fri. or Sat. nights. If you are lucky, you may come across a ceilidh (pronounced 'kay-lay'), a local dance, usually held in the village hall, where visitors are made welcome. See **Music**, **What's On**.

Oban: Pop: 7000. Tourist Information (all year), Argyll Sq., tel: 0631-63122. Oban is an important railway terminus and ferry port, and a lively centre for tourism and yachting. It has been a popular resort since Victorian times, and is well supplied with accommodation, restaurants, shops, sports facilities and outdoor activities. Caledonian Macbrayne, Railway Pier, tel: 0631-62285, runs car ferries to Mull, Lismore, Coll, Tiree, Colonsay, Barra and South Uist, and also offers cruises to many islands, including Iona and Staffa. There is a sandy beach at Ganavan, 2 miles north of the town, beyond the remains of 13thC Dunollie Castle.

Prominent on the skyline above the town centre is McCaig's Folly, a circular tower reminiscent of the Colosseum in Rome. This circular stone structure was built between 1890 and 1900 at the behest of local banker John Stuart McCaig to ease unemployment in the area. It can be reached by walking up Craigard St, towards the north end of George St (the main street that runs along the harbour front). The view across to Mull is excellent. Another good viewpoint is Pulpit Hill, above the south end of the harbour, which can be reached by following Albany St from Argyll Sq. Although Oban is principally used as a centre for exploring the surrounding area, there are a number of attractions within the town itself. The Highland Discovery Centre (1000-1730 Sun.-Fri., 1000-1330 Sat.; 95p, child 55p) in George St has audio-visual shows and films about the Scottish Highlands, while the World in Miniature (1000-1730 Mon.-Sat., 1200-1730 Sun., Easter-mid Oct.; £1, child 70p) on nearby North Pier houses an exhibition of the work of Britain's best miniaturists, with displays of tiny rooms, models, dioramas, etc. The Oban Glassworks (0900-1700 Mon.-Fri.; free), run by Caithness Glass, at Lochavullin Estate, Lochavullin Rd, has self-guided tours of the factory, where you can see glass-blowers in action before browsing in the factory shop. See **EXCURSIONS 4B & 5**, **Ferries**.

Opening Times: These are general opening times and may be subject to variation. Most towns have an early-closing day, usually Tue., Wed. or Thu., when shops are closed all afternoon.
Banks – 0930-1230, 1330-1530 Mon.-Fri. & 1630-1830 Thu. An increasing number of banks now stay open at lunchtime and in city centres some branches open on Sat. morning.
Bars – 1100-2300 Mon.-Sat., 1200-1430, 1800-2200 Sun.
Historic Scotland (see **A-Z**) sites – 0930-1900 Mon.-Sat., 1400-1900 Sun. (April-Sep.); 0930-1600 Mon.-Sat., 1400-1600 Sun. (Oct.-Mar.).
Offices – 0900-1700 Mon.-Fri.
Post offices – 0900-1730 Mon.-Fri., 0900-1230 Sat.
Shops – 0900-1730 Mon.-Sat. In popular tourist areas in summer, you may find places open later, and on Sun. too.

Orkney: See **EXCURSION 6**.

St. Magnus' Cathedral, Orkney

Parking: City centre parking can be a problem. In Glasgow there are multi-storey car parks at Anderston Cross, George St, Mitchell St, St. Enoch Centre and Waterloo St; in Edinburgh, at Castle Terr. (off Lothian Rd) and the St. James' Centre (east end of Princes St). There are parking meters on many streets (30 min for 20p). A single yellow line at the kerb means no parking during daytime; a double yellow line means no parking at any time. Traffic wardens are plentiful and vigilant. Penalties for illegal parking range from a £12 fine to the towing away and impounding of the vehicle. See **Driving**.

Passports & Customs: A valid passport (or identity card for some EC visitors) is required by foreign citizens visiting the UK. No visas are necessary for EC citizens, Commonwealth citizens (inc. Australia, Canada and New Zealand) and citizens of the USA and the Republic of South Africa. At customs, if you have goods to declare over and above your duty-free allowances, you should follow the Red channel (you must also declare anything you intend to leave or sell in the UK); if you have nothing to declare, follow the Green channel (which is subject to spot checks by customs officers). There are no restrictions on the amount of money you may take into or out of the country.

Perth: Pop: 42,000. Tourist Information (all year), 45 High St, tel: 0738-38353. Built on the banks of the River Tay, the 'Fair City' of Perth sits at the 'Crossroads of Scotland' and was the capital for a time. The Church of St. John, just off the High St, gave the town its original name of St. Johnstoun (the local football club retains the name), and it was from the pulpit here that John Knox (see **A-Z**) delivered his famous sermon denouncing Catholic 'idolatry'. The Fair Maid's House (1100-1600) is the oldest building in the town and now houses an art gallery and a shop selling contemporary Scottish crafts. The Regimental Museum of the Black Watch (1000-1630 Mon.-Sat., 1400-1630 Sun.; free), a famous Highland regiment, is in Balhousie Castle, at North Inch Park. Nearby Scone Palace (0930-1700; £3, child £2, family £10), 2 miles out of town on the A 93, is built on the site of Scone Abbey, where for 700 years the kings of Scotland were crowned on the Stone of Destiny. The stone's origin is unclear, but it has been linked with

Scone Palace

both Jacob's Pillow at Bethel and the Stone of Destiny at Tara in Ireland. In 1297 Edward I removed the stone to Westminster, where it remains to this day beneath the coronation throne. The palace today contains collections of 18thC French furniture, porcelain, ivories, clocks and needlework. On the western edge of Perth, on the A 85 towards Crieff, is the splendid 15thC Huntingtower Castle (0930-1900 Mon.-Sat., 1400-1900 Sun., until 1600 Oct.-Mar.; 60p, child 30p), whose fine architecture includes a remarkable painted ceiling. On the A 85 to the east of the city are the superb Branklyn Gardens (0930-sun-set; £1.40, child 70p) and the Fairways Heavy Horse Centre (1000-1800 April-Sep.; free), a working and steeding centre for Clydesdales. See **EXCURSION 11**.

Petrol: Petrol is widely available throughout the country; unleaded petrol is indicated by a green sign. However, service stations can be few and far between in the north and west, so keep your tank well topped up. In certain parts of the northwest, petrol stations are closed on Sun. (see **Customs**). See **Driving**.

Picts: The Picts were the original inhabitants of northern Scotland, encountered by the invading Romans in the 1st and 2ndC AD. Little is known about them, but it seems they were an amalgamation of the Celtic tribes who had colonized the east coast. They mostly inhabited the areas round Fife, the Tay and Dunkeld (see **EXCURSION 11**), and fought the occupying Romans for more than a century, their repeated attacks on the invaders resulting in the building of the Antonine Wall (see **A-Z**). The delicate stone carvings and silverwork that they left behind belie their traditional image as barbarians.

Pitlochry: See **EXCURSION 11**.

Police: British police wear a dark uniform and black peaked cap with a chequered band. They are not armed and you will generally find them friendly and helpful in their dealings with visitors. In an emergency, tel: 999 and ask for the police. See **Crime & Theft**, **Emergency Numbers**.

Post Offices: These are indicated by a red sign with yellow lettering. In small towns and villages the post office is often located in the village store. Letter boxes are painted bright red and display the times of collections. Post offices sell stamps for letters and parcels, and there is often a vending machine outside which will sell stamps when the office is closed. Within the UK, letters can be sent either first or second class: first class is slightly more expensive but should guarantee next-day delivery; second-class mail may take several days to arrive. First-class letters up to 20 g to UK addresses, 22p; airmail to EC countries, 22p, rest of Europe, 26p; airmail letters up to 10 g, rest of the world, 37p. You can receive mail addressed c/o Poste Restante at the main post office in any town. You will need your passport or other identification when you go to collect anything. The main post office in Edinburgh is at 2-4 Waterloo Pl., EH1 1AA, and that in Glasgow at 1-5 George Sq., G2 (0830-1800 Mon.-Fri., 0830-1230 Sat.). See **Opening Times**.

Public Holidays: 1-2 Jan. (New Year); Good Fri.; 1st Mon. in May (May Day Bank Holiday); last Mon. in May (Spring Bank Holiday); 1st Mon. in Aug. (August Bank Holiday); 25 Dec. (Christmas Day); 26 Dec. (Boxing Day). Bank holidays are usually observed only by banks, and most shops and offices remain open.

Falls of Dochart, Killin

Dunrobin Castle

Balmoral Castle

Blair Castle

Cawdor Castle

Railways: ScotRail services connect Glasgow and Edinburgh to London and all principal mainland towns in Scotland. The main lines north from Glasgow and Edinburgh run through Perth and on to Inverness, one via Aviemore, the other via Aberdeen. Branch lines continue to Kyle of Lochalsh (ferry to Skye), and to Wick and Thurso (ferry to Orkney). From Glasgow, a line runs southwest through Ayr to Stranraer (ferry to Northern Ireland), and the scenic West Highland line (see **Fort William**) runs through the mountains to termini at Oban (ferries to Mull and the Outer Hebrides) and Mallaig (ferries to Skye and the Small Isles). InterCity services have buffet, restaurant car and sleeper facilities. London to Edinburgh takes about 5 hr and the standard single fare is £53, but there are special return tickets which are much cheaper: a SuperSaver (not valid for travel on Fri. and certain bank holidays) is £54 return, and an Apex ticket (limited availability, must be booked at least seven days in advance) is only £44 return. From Glasgow to Fort William is £17.50 single, £23 SuperSaver return. From Edinburgh to Inverness is £15.50 single, £21 SuperSaver return. If you plan to do a lot of travelling by rail, you might consider buying a Freedom of Scotland rover ticket. These tickets are available from all major railway stations in Scotland and England, and from travel agents, and are valid for unlimited travel on all ScotRail services from Berwick and Carlisle in the south to Wick and Thurso in the north. A seven-day ticket costs £56, a 15-day ticket £92. Cheaper rover tickets are available for limited areas, e.g. seven days' unlimited travel on the West Highland line only costs £28. Details can be obtained from information desks at main railway stations. Travelpass tickets (see **Transport**) are valid on certain ScotRail services. For details of ScotRail timetables and fares from Edinburgh, tel: 031-5562451; and from Glasgow, tel: 041-2042844.

Reformation, The: The Reformation was a religious and political revolution that swept through Europe in the 16thC. It began by challenging the authority of the Roman Catholic Church and ended in the establishment of the Protestant Church. Its effects were particularly strongly felt in Scotland, which suffered much violence and destruction during this period, and resulted in what had previously been a Catholic country subsequently becoming an overwhelmingly Protestant nation with a strong Calvinist tradition. See **Knox**.

Rennie, John (1761-1821): John Rennie was born at Phantassie House in East Linton, East Lothian. He went to Edinburgh University and by the time he was 30 was one of Britain's most celebrated consultant engineers. In England he built Waterloo and Southwark bridges, the new London Docks and supervised the draining of the Fens. In Scotland one of his finest bridges was built in Kelso (see **EXCURSION 13**) in 1800. A workaholic, he died aged 60 and is buried in St. Paul's Cathedral, London.

Robert the Bruce (1274-1329): Robert the Bruce was one of Scotland's most famous and best-loved kings. He is remembered for having inflicted a crippling defeat against the English at Bannockburn (see **Stirling**), and assuring Scotland's independence at a time when it was in danger of being reduced to the status of an English county. Bruce, a descendant of King David I of Scotland, asserted his claim to the throne in 1306, at a time when Scotland was being ruled by Edward I of England (known as 'The Hammer of the Scots'). He disposed of a rival claimant, Sir John Comyn, by stabbing him to death in Greyfriars Friary, Dumfries (see **EXCURSION 1**), a crime for which he was excommunicated, then had himself crowned King of Scotland at Scone (see **Perth**). His campaign to drive the English out went badly at first, and he spent a year in exile on Rathlin Island, in Ireland, living in a cave. Here, legend has it that he watched a spider struggling to complete its web, and was inspired by its persistence to return to Scotland to try again (there are a number of 'Bruce's Caves', all of which claim to be the place where he watched the spider). He won a series of victories and his support increased: he was now backed by the Church, the

French king and many of the clans. His greatest victory came in June 1314, at Bannockburn, when his army, although outnumbered three to one, defeated a force of 20,000 English sent by Edward II. Bruce was confirmed as king in 1320, and in 1328 Edward III formally granted independence to Scotland under the Treaty of Northampton. Bruce died in 1329 and was buried in Dunfermline Abbey (see **EXCURSION 12**), but his heart was carried on a crusade to the Holy Land by his friend and fellow warrior, Sir James Douglas. Unfortunately, all Bruce's gains were short-lived – the English king broke the Treaty of Northampton in 1333 and invaded Scotland again.

Rob Roy (1671-1734): Robert Macgregor, popularly known as Rob Roy (Red Robert) because of his flaming red hair, was a cattle-thief and outlaw who roamed the hills of the central Highlands, and was romanticized by Sir Walter Scott (see **A-Z**) and others into a Robin Hood-type figure. His home territory was the area north of the Trossachs (see **EXCURSION 3**).

St. Andrews: Pop: 11,300. Full services. Tourist Information (all year), South St, tel: 0334-72021. A bustling university town crammed with historic and ancient buildings. St. Andrews Cathedral (0930-1900 Mon.-Sat., 1400-1900 Sun.; 60p, child 30p) is partly ruined though it's still an impressive structure. Its museum contains various religious artefacts, including a stone coffin. From the museum you can enter the church of St. Regulus (St. Rule's Tower). The 108 ft-tall tower affords panoramic views over the town. Behind the tower lies St. Mary-on-the-Rock, the foundations of the Celtic church of the Culdees that fell into disuse as the cathedral flourished. Founded in 1200 and overlooking the sea, St. Andrews Castle (same admission details as the cathedral) is noted for its underground tunnels, examples of the siege mining techniques used in bygone ages, and the Bottle Dungeon, cut 24 ft into solid rock. The St. Andrews Preservation Trust Museum (1400-1700 Mon.-Fri., July & Aug.; free) on North St outlines local history. The West Port Arch (at the west end of South St) leads into the old town with its 15thC churches and university colleges. Follow North St out of town with the Royal and Ancient Golf Club on the right; down Golf Pl.

Founded in 1754 it is the head-quarters of the world game. There are four courses where visitors can play, including the famed Old Course. There is also an 11 mile walk southwest along the coast to Crail. See **EXCURSION 12**.

St. Columba (c.521–597): Columba was an adventurous Irish monk who sailed to Scotland and founded a church and monastery on the island of Iona (see **EXCURSION 5**) in AD 563. He and his team of missionaries spread Christianity through northern and western Scotland, and founded a number of churches and religious communities.

St. Ninian (c.360–c.432): St. Ninian was a Briton whose family was converted to Christianity, possibly by invading Roman soldiers. He received his religious education in Rome and returned to found a church and religious school – the first Christian church in Scotland – at Whithorn (see **EXCURSION 1**) in Galloway (the name comes from the ancient English, *hwit aerne* meaning 'white building'). He is the first recorded Christian missionary to Scotland.

Whithorn Dig   Ruthwell Cross

Scott, Sir Walter (1771-1832): Sir Walter Scott, one of Scotland's most famous writers, was born and educated in Edinburgh, and in 1786 joined his father's law firm. He began as a poet, and by the time he was appointed Sheriff of Selkirk in 1799 he was already well established (*The Lady of the Lake*). But it is for his historical novels – *Rob Roy*, *Ivanhoe* and the 'Waverley Novels' – that he is best remembered. A great popularizer of Scotland's historical and cultural past, he was at the forefront of the Scottish Romantic movement which revived a national awareness that had been in danger of extinction after the years of oppression that followed the Covenanters' (see **A-Z**) movement and the Jacobite rebellion (see **Bonnie Prince Charlie**). In 1811 he bought a small farmhouse and spent the next 14 years and £25,000 converting it into the mansion of Abbotsford (see **EXCURSION 13**). The bankruptcy of his publisher in 1826 almost ruined Scott. He died six years later, having practically written himself into the grave to make sufficient money.

Shetland: See **EXCURSION 9**.

Skye, Isle of: See **EXCURSION 5**.

Small Isles: The Small Isles are the Inner Hebridean islands of Eigg, Muck, Rhum and Canna that lie a little to the south of Skye. They can be reached by ferry from Mallaig (see **EXCURSION 5**). The largest is Rhum (with an area of 64 sq. miles), a wild and mountainous island rising to 2659 ft, of great interest to naturalists, bird-watchers, geologists and hill walkers. It is a National Nature Reserve and anyone planning to stay overnight must seek permission to camp from the Reserve Office, The

Whitehouse, Rhum PH43 4RR, tel: 0687-2026. Luxury accommodation is available at Kinloch Castle, near the ferry landing, a magnificent residence built in 1901 by Sir George Bullough, then owner of the island. Eigg (5 miles by 2.5 miles) is notable for its distinctive, rocky hill, the Scuir of Eigg, and the Singing Sands of Camus Sgiolaig. The sand on this beach in the northwest of the island squeaks or 'sings' when you walk on it, or sometimes even when it is blown by the wind. Muck and Canna are smaller and flatter, with sparse populations and no services, but provide pleasant and secluded walking.

Smith, Adam (1723-90): Born in Kirkcaldy in Fife, Adam Smith is renowned as the father of the science of political economy. His book *The Wealth of Nations*, published in 1776, laid out a philosophy claiming that wealth was dependent on labour, and that although all people were individuals, they worked together unconsciously for the common good. He believed that happiness should be the central tenet of political economy. He died in 1790 regretting that he had achieved so little with his life.

Sports: Participator sports: Scotland is the birthplace of golf, and while many visitors will want to pit themselves against the world-famous courses at St. Andrews, Turnberry and Gleneagles, there are more than 400 courses to choose from throughout the country, many in very scenic locations. The Old Course at St. Andrews must be booked at least two months in advance, but the great majority of courses are relatively uncrowded, and the green fees remarkably cheap. Scotland can boast of having more golf courses per head of population than anywhere else in the world. *Scotland: Home of Golf* is available free from the STB (see **Tourist Information**).

Angling for trout and salmon is excellent, and often ridiculously cheap compared with England. Although salmon fishing on famous rivers like the Tweed and the Tay can be extortionately expensive, you can fish for salmon and trout at many locations for no more than a few pounds, and occasionally for free. In many places, permits can be obtained at the local Tourist Information office: if not they will be able to tell you where to get one. More details are included in the booklet *Scotland for*

Fishing, which is available free from the Scottish Tourist Board.
Walking and hill walking are very popular in Scotland (see **Walking**),
and other popular outdoor pursuits which can be enjoyed at many
locations all over Scotland include horse riding (around £6.50 per hr),
mountain biking (see **Bicycle & Motorcycle Hire**) and sailing (hire of a
16 ft Wayfarer sailing dinghy, £26 per day).

There is excellent scuba diving in the waters off the west coast and in
world-famous Scapa Flow, Orkney. Beginners can arrange five-day
courses of instruction (around £250) at dive schools in Oban, Fort
William and a number of other locations.

In winter, the ski slopes at Aviemore, Glenshee, the Lecht, Glencoe and
Aonach Mor draw skiers from all over Britain: instruction and equipment hire are available. Scotland's national winter sport is curling, but
you can try your hand all year round in one of the country's many
indoor ice rinks; skating, of course, is available too.

Spectator sports: The country's most popular spectator sport is football. Games are played on Sat. afternoon and Wed. evening in the season (Aug.-May). The best-known teams are Glasgow's Rangers and Celtic. In Feb. and Mar. you can attend two of the Rugby Union matches in the Five Nations Tournament, which are played at Murrayfield Stadium in Edinburgh, but buy your tickets well in advance.

Horse racing is popular and there are several well-known Scottish meetings, including the Ayr Gold Cup in Sep.

Other big events in the sporting calendar are the Scottish Six-Day Motorcycle Trials (May), the RSAC Scottish Rally (June) and the Scottish Open Golf Championship (July). And all through the summer months there are the Highland Games. These are local gatherings where competitions include Highland dancing, piping, athletics, tossing the caber (a section of tree trunk) and throwing the hammer. The most famous is the Braemar Highland Gathering in Sep., which is occasionally attended by members of the royal family.

Staffa: The little island of Staffa lies off the west coast of Mull, and can be reached by boat trip from Oban (see **A-Z**), or from Dervaig or Fionnphort on Mull (see **EXCURSION 5**). It is composed of basalt lava, which on the south and west coasts is displayed in spectacular cliffs of hexagonal columns, formed by the contraction of the lava as it cooled. The island is famous for Fingal's Cave, a sea-filled cavern which penetrates almost 230 ft into the cliffs, with a roof 65 ft high. The composer Mendelssohn visited the cave in 1829 and was inspired to write his famous *Hebrides Overture*.

Stevenson, Robert Louis (1850-94): This world-famous writer was born in Edinburgh, into a family famed as engineers and builders of lighthouses (see **Coll & Tiree**), and lived for about 30 years at 17 Heriot Row, in the city's New Town. He qualified as an advocate at Edinburgh University in 1867, but made his name as a writer with such works as *A Child's Garden of Verse*, *Treasure Island*, *Kidnapped* and *The Strange Case of Dr Jekyll and Mr Hyde*. He also wrote the words to the well-known *Skye Boat Song*. He died in Samoa in the South Pacific and is buried there.

Stirling: Pop: 38,600. Full services. Tourist Information (all year), Dumbarton Rd, tel: 0786-75019. Dating back to the Middle Ages, Stirling Castle (0930-1700, last entry 1615; £2, child £1) dominates not just the town but the whole of central Scotland. It's been called 'the key to Scotland' and as such its possession has been the subject of conflict in the past. On the Castle Esplanade there is the Landmark Visitor Centre which recounts over 700 years of the town's history. Particularly noteworthy are the Chapel Royal where Mary, Queen of Scots (see **A-Z**) was crowned, the Great Hall and the Argyll and Sutherland Highlanders Regimental Museum. Plainly visible from the ramparts is the Wallace Monument on the other side of town which commemorates William Wallace (see **A-Z**), the Scots 'guerilla'. (Follow the A 9 to Causewayhead and then the signs on the A 91 to reach the monument.) In the town see the Church of the Holy Rude on St. John St, the only church in Scotland to have seen a coronation (James VI) and still be in use, and Stirling Bridge. Built c.1400, this was the only route north from Stirling for nearly 300 years. Two miles south of the town is the Bannockburn Heritage Centre (1000-1800; £1, child 50p) which details the events leading up to the Battle of Bannockburn (1314) and the battle itself, which the Scots won. It established Robert the Bruce (see **A-Z**) as King of Scotland. See **EXCURSIONS 3 & 11**.

Telephones & Telegrams: Public payphones are common throughout the country. The older blue payphones accept only 2p, 10p and 50p coins, while the newer, single-slot machines, which are gradually replacing the older ones, accept all coins except 1p. Minimum charge is 10p. Instructions for use are clearly displayed in the 'phone booth. You can make local, long-distance and international calls from all telephones, either by dialling direct, or through the operator (UK operator, tel: 100; international operator, tel: 155). For UK directory enquiries, dial 192; for international directory enquiries, tel: 153. If you have any difficulties making a call, contact the operator by dialling 100. Telephones with a green Phonecard sign can only be used with a plastic card available from post offices and newsagents in £1, £5 and £10 versions. In the UK, a 'collect' call is known as a reverse-charge call. To make an international call, dial 010 followed by the country code (USA and Canada 1, Australia 61, New Zealand 64, France 33, West Germany 49), then the area code minus the initial zero, and finally the number. Full instructions can be found in any telephone directory. The cheapest time to make UK calls is 1800-0600 weekdays, and during the weekend. A local call costs 10p for 3 min. A similar call to London costs 30p, to France and Germany £1.10, to the USA £2, and to Australia £3.

All telegrams must be dictated by telephone; there is no longer a traditional counter service. Tel: 100 and ask for Telemessage (for UK and USA) or International Telegrams (for the rest of the world).

Time Differences: The British Isles use Greenwich Mean Time (GMT) late Oct.-late Mar., and British Summer Time (GMT plus 1 hr) April-Oct. At noon in Scotland in summer it is: 1300 in Paris and Berlin; 0700 in New York and Montreal; 0400 in Los Angeles and Vancouver; 2100 in Sydney; and 2300 in Auckland.

Tipping: Hotels and restaurants often include a service charge in your bill. Where service is not included, it is customary to leave a tip of 10-15% to waiting staff. Porters expect 30-50p per bag and taxi drivers often get 10-15% of the fare. Tipping is not expected in theatres, cinemas and petrol stations.

Toilets: Scotland is plentifully supplied with well-maintained public toilets. You will find them in bus and railway stations, town centres, public parks, museums, art galleries and other tourist attractions. There is usually no charge for their use.

Tourist Information: The Scottish Tourist Board (STB) runs more than 150 Tourist Information offices all over the country, many of which are mentioned in the **EXCURSIONS**. They will reserve accommodation (see **A-Z**), issue free maps and leaflets, and offer help with any enquiry you may have. Opening hours are generally 0900-1700 daily.

Most are open only Easter-Oct., but main centres are open all year round. Information and special publications can be obtained from the STB head office, 23 Ravelston Terr., Edinburgh EH4 3EU, tel: 031-3322433 (postal and telephone enquiries only). There is also an STB office at 19 Cockspur St, London SW1 5LB, tel: 071-9308661.

Transport: A comprehensive network of air, bus, train and ferry routes serves most of Scotland, making public transport a viable means of seeing much of the country. All services are comfortable and easy to use. Buses are slower than trains over long distances, but are considerably cheaper and cover a much wider area. For visitors planning to travel extensively on public transport in the Highlands and Islands, a special Travelpass ticket would be a good investment. Available only between 1 Mar. and 31 Oct. Travelpass is valid for journeys north from Glasgow and Edinburgh on scheduled ScotRail services, Scottish Bus Group and Scottish Citylink buses, Caledonian Macbrayne ferries and the P&O Scrabster–Stromness (Orkney) ferry. Included with the ticket are free timetables and maps. These tickets can be purchased at certain main-line railway stations and travel centres in Scotland and London, and cost £65 for seven days or £90 for 15 days in the peak season (June-Sep.); the off-peak prices are £40 and £60 respectively. For details, contact Highlands and Islands Travelpass, Hi-Line, Dingwall, Ross-shire IV15 9SL, tel: 0349-63434. See **Airports**, **Buses**, **Ferries**, **Railways**.

Traveller's Cheques: See **Money**.

Wade, Gen. George (1673-1748): Wade was an English army officer sent to Scotland in 1724 to help pacify the clans, but is best remembered for the 250 miles of military roads and the 42 bridges that he built between 1725 and 1740, which helped to open up the Highlands.

Near The Storr, Skye

Walking: Scotland's beautiful countryside provides excellent walking for visitors at all levels of ability, from a 30 min stroll along a well-marked footpath, through moderate hill walks to multi-day expeditions into some of Britain's wildest mountains. There are a few signposted long-distance footpaths, notably the West Highland Way, from Glasgow to Fort William (95 miles), and the Southern Upland Way, from Portpatrick to Cockburnspath (212 miles). A number of easy walks are described in the EXCURSIONS, and Tourist Information offices provide full details of local walks. Useful publications include *Scotland: Walks and Trails* (£2.80) and *Scotland: Hill Walking* (£2.60), available from bookshops or direct from the STB (see **Tourist Information**).

WARNING: Scotland's hills can be dangerous. Weather conditions can change very quickly and snow can fall on the high summits at any time of year. Anyone planning a walking trip above valley level should be fully equipped with proper walking boots, warm clothes, waterproofs, map, compass, first-aid kit, whistle and plenty of spare food. Leave a note describing your proposed route and expected time of return with a responsible person.

Falls of Shin

Wallace, William (c.1270-1305):

Wallace is one of the great heroes of Scotland's long struggle against England. Scotland was under English rule when William Wallace's wife was assaulted and killed by English troops stationed at Lanark. In retaliation Wallace murdered the Sheriff of Lanark and was declared an outlaw. A band of supporters gathered about him and he began a campaign to drive the English out of Scotland. His army used guerilla tactics, living and training in hiding, and making surprise attacks on English-held castles and barracks. This uprising culminated in a victory for Wallace at the Battle of Stirling Bridge in 1297, and the capture of Stirling Castle (see **Stirling**). He ruled as Guardian of Scotland for a year before Edward I sent an army north which defeated the Scots at the Battle of Falkirk. However, it took another six years and a similar number of invasions, which ravaged the Border country, before Edward finally recaptured Stirling. After Falkirk, Wallace remained in hiding and continued his guerilla war. In 1305, he was betrayed to the English and was taken to London where he was castrated, hung, drawn and quartered. His head was placed on a pike on London Bridge and his severed limbs were distributed round the towns of Scotland as a warning. Wallace's activities foreshadowed Robert the Bruce's (see **A-Z**) more successful campaign.

Stirling Castle

Edinburgh Festival

What's On: There are separate monthly listings brochures published in each Scottish Tourist Board region. They are generally titled *What's On in . . .* and can be picked up free at Tourist Information offices, hotels, restaurants, etc. There is also a monthly national listing, *What's On Scotland*, also free. These cover exhibitions, theatre, music, tours, special events, museums, eating out, etc. In Glasgow and Edinburgh there are more detailed weekly listings in the Sat. editions of local newspapers and in the fortnightly magazine *The List* (90p from newsagents), which covers cinema, theatre, music, art and sport. See **Events, Newspapers**.

Whisky Trail: Beginning at Tomintoul (see **EXCURSION 10**), this special tourist trail leads through eight distilleries – Tamnavulin-Glenlivet, Glenfiddich, Strathisla, Glen Grant, Cardhu, Tamdhu, Glenfarclas and The Glenlivet. All provide audio-visual displays, a tour of the distillery and a free dram. Bring your own Alka-Seltzer! For more information pick up a leaflet from the local Tourist Information offices.

Wick: Pop: 8000. Tourist Information (all year), Whitechapel Rd (off High St), tel: 0955-2596. Wick is a pleasant fishing port ranged around the bay that gives it its name (*vik* is Old Norse for 'bay'). Places of interest include the award-winning Wick Heritage Centre (1000-1230, 1400-1700 Mon.-Sat., June-Sep.; £1, child 50p) at 20 Bank Row, a museum of local history and particularly of the herring-fishing industry (Wick was once the world's largest herring-fishing port). On the south side of town is the Caithness Glass factory, which offers self-guided tours of the glassworks (0900-1200, 1230-1630 Mon.-Fri.; free) and a factory shop (0900-1700 Mon.-Fri., 0900-1300 Sat.). A few miles further south on the coast is 12thC Old Wick Castle, reached by a pleasant 10 min cliff-top walk. It is one of Scotland's oldest stone-built castles and occupies a spectacular situation on a cliff above the sea. North of the town, near the lighthouse on Noss Head, are two more ruined castles, Castle Girnigoe and Castle Sinclair. See **EXCURSION 7**.

**Wolf of Badenoch
(d.1394):** Otherwise
known as Alexander Stewart, Earl of Buchan, this violent natural son of
King Robert II terrorized the countryside. After his excommunication in
1390 by the Bishop of Elgin for leaving his lawful wife for another
woman, he destroyed the town and its cathedral (see **EXCURSION 8**). The
'Wolf' later did penance for his atrocious deeds at Elgin's Mercat Cross
and an armoured effigy in Dunkeld Cathedral (see **EXCURSION 11**) is
thought to be his.

Youth Hostels: The Scottish Youth Hostels Association (SYHA) has
over 80 youth hostels all over Scotland, ranging from large, modern
establishments to small cottages with only a handful of beds, several
miles' walk from the nearest road. Facilities and prices vary considerably, the latter from £2.25 to £4.25 per night. You must be a member of
the SYHA or of your own national Youth Hostel Association. For further
information contact the SYHA head office at 7 Glebe Cres., Stirling
FK8 2JA, tel: 0786-72821. Membership costs £5 per year and you can
join at most hostels; a passport-size photo is required.